COLUMBIA COLLEGE CHICAGO

C0-DKM-532

JUL 0 7 2010

The Resonance of a Small Voice

COLUMBIA COLLEGE LIBRARY
600 S. MICHIGAN AVENUE
CHICAGO, IL 60605

The Resonance of a Small Voice:
William Walton and the Violin Concerto
in England between 1900 and 1940

By

Paolo Petrocelli

CAMBRIDGE
SCHOLARS

P U B L I S H I N G

The Resonance of a Small Voice:
William Walton and the Violin Concerto in England between 1900 and 1940,
by Paolo Petrocelli

This book first published 2010

Cambridge Scholars Publishing

12 Back Chapman Street, Newcastle upon Tyne, NE6 2XX, UK

British Library Cataloguing in Publication Data
A catalogue record for this book is available from the British Library

Copyright © 2010 by Paolo Petrocelli

All rights for this book reserved. No part of this book may be reproduced, stored in a retrieval system,
or transmitted, in any form or by any means, electronic, mechanical, photocopying, recording or
otherwise, without the prior permission of the copyright owner.

ISBN (10): 1-4438-1721-X, ISBN (13): 978-1-4438-1721-9

To my mother

TABLE OF CONTENTS

ACKNOWLEDGEMENTS

Particular thanks to:

Philip Gossett, for having encouraged me to discover the value of musicological research.

Lady Susana Walton, the William Walton Foundation, the Walton Trust for their full and kind availability.

Hans Werner Henze, Salvatore Accardo, James Ehnes, Matthew Jones, Fenella Humphreys for having wanted to enrich this work with their reflections.

Oxford University Press, for permitting the reproduction of copyrighted material.

My friend Jordan De Maio for having translated this book from Italian.

Emiliano Ricciardi for having edited the translation.

My entire family, who have supported my work and studies with affection and wisdom.

PREFACE

This text represents both a study and a historical musicological analysis of Sir William Walton's Violin Concerto, treating the form of the violin concerto, in general, in England as it developed between 1900 and 1940, taking into consideration the works of Charles Villiers Stanford, Edward Elgar, Samuel Coleridge-Taylor, Frederick Delius, Ralph Vaughan Williams, Arthur Somervell, Arnold Bax and Benjamin Britten.

The study is divided into three parts:

-   The Violin Concerto in England between 1900-1920: Stanford[1], Elgar, Coleridge-Taylor, Delius.

-   The Violin Concerto in England between 1920 and 1940: Vaughan Williams, Somervell, Bax, Britten.

-   William Walton's Violin Concerto

The book opens with a brief description of the form of the Violin Concerto between the 19th and 20th centuries in Europe. This description intends to provide both a familiarity with the base characteristics of this musical form during the period under examination and the beginning of a comparison between different national compositional styles.

Each individual section is introduced with a portrait of the historical musical character in England (during the respective period) and presents, after a biographical exposition of the composers, a formal structural, harmonic and aesthetic analysis (this analysis is embedded within a general discussion of the concertos themselves). In addition one study of the technical and interpretative aspects of the concerto and one reflection on the relationship between composer and performer form part of the analysis.. At the closing of each section a comparative overview is also given.

The first and the second parts are developed, entirely, in relation to the third, which treats, exclusively and with significant depth, Sir William

---

[1] Concerto D Major Op.74 (1899), last concerto of the 19th century in England.

Walton's Violin Concerto, the work to which the greatest attention is devoted.

The appendix provides various unpublished texts concerning some of the concertos treated (with particular reference to Walton's) that were gathered during research. It is hoped that these will prove useful in enriching and completing a reflection, begun in the book, on the decidedly performative and interpretative aspect of violin music produced by British composers in the first half of the 20th century.

Currently there are no modern texts that approach the violin concertos of this period in an exhaustive way. This text proposes to fill the gap, drawing the attention of scholars, musicologists and musicians to the appeal of this repertoire, composed of works of great artistic value that have been, for too long, unjustly forgotten.

The volume will be useful for university and conservatory students, musicologists, composers, violinists and musicians in general in as much as it treats, in specialized yet accessible language, the aspects of the concerto that are of interest to the author.

The study is enriched by the presence of unpublished documents (letters and essays written by both the composers themselves and by those to whom the concertos were dedicated), that will help to illuminate the myriad cultural and personal circumstances that fed and gave life to these great works.

THE CONCERTO FOR VIOLIN AND ORCHESTRA

Here an analysis of the concerto for violin and orchestra, as the form developed in England between 1900 and 1940, will be presented. In beginning an analysis such as this, musicological in nature, it is useful to make some observations concerning the concerto as a form, in Europe, in the 19th and 20th centuries. Doing so will permit us to evaluate, through a "comparative" lense, both the different national styles that characterize the form and the various compositional approaches that have and continue to influence it.[1]

The classical period that spanned the end of the 1700's and the beginning of the 1800's was a period of intense change. During this period the violin concerto adhered to the principles of the sonata form, which gradually substituted the baroque form of the ritornello. It was also a period in which the presence of the rondo as a third movement and double exposition were definitively affirmed. Cadenzas were standardized and the use of the continuo disappeared. Orchestral accompaniment usually presented itself in a homophonic style, providing a finer tessitura, especially during solos.

Violin melodies became, in great part, *cantabile* and scoring for the instrument's higher registers became more frequent as a result of the perfecting of technique, which opened up new technical possibilities. With the advent of the modern bow in 1780 (developed by Francois Tourte), particular attention was paid to purity of sound and to the realization of sustained sound; moreover, with the introduction of a new type of chinrest the left hand's ability was greatly enhanced. This also allowed for more complex scores.

From the second half of the 19th century, on the basis of typically Romantic expressions and idioms, new changes were brought to the concerto form. The form of the ritornello was definitively abandoned for the sonata and cyclic form, with a notable formal expansion of the first

---

[1] Arnaldo Bonaventura Storia del violino, dei violinisti e della musica per violino, Ed.Lampi di Stampa; Robin Stowell The Cambridge Companion to the Violin, Cambridge University Press; Mark Katz The Violin: A Research and Information Guide, Routledge; Michael Thomas Roeder A history of the concerto Amadeus Press.

movement, especially in the final codas. The use of the double exposition was also abandoned. The slow second movement, initially tied to the finale and conceived as its introduction, became an automous movement.

The finale, incorporating national elements, could utilize folk melodies and dance rhythms and present itself in *scherzo* form. The cadenzas were, by then, an integral part of the concerto form and often were composed by the authors themselves. The solo, now increasingly characterized by virtuosity, often accompanied the tutti - one could say that the lyrical possibilities of the violin were emphasized. During the first Romantic period orchestral interventions were reduced to a minimum while the second half of the century favored a symphonic use of the orchestra.

Scores in general, which preferred minor keys, provided for the presence of chromaticism and modulations in distant tones by means both of rhythmic designs that were growing more complex and by the frequent use of syncopation and changes in tempo. Violin technique went further in its utilization of effects, such as harmonics, false harmonics, the left-handed pizzicato and through bow strokes such as the spiccato, the ricochet and the picchettato.

The wide repertoire of concertos for violin and orchestra produced in the 19th century is constituted of works coming from three different groups of composers. The first of these is represented by those musicians who were strongly tied to the traditional form of the classical period. This form saw its maximum expression in the violin concertos of Louis Spohr (1784-1859) and Felix Mendelssohn (1809-1847). In particular Mendelssohn's Concerto for Violin and Orchestra Op. 64, composed between 1838 and 1844, surely one of the most fascinating works of the entire repertoire for violin, embodies through its "cantabilità" the pureness of its themes, the energy and the virtuosity of the solo part, and the emotional sensibility of the Romantic artist.

The German composer, even if tied to the three movement form of the classic concerto, introduced the idea of unity, calling for a performance with pauses between one movement and another and so tending towards a "cyclic" form.

The second group is represented by composer-violinists such as Niccolò Paganini (1784-1840), Charles de Beriot (1802-1870), Henryk Wieniawski (1835-1880), Henry Vieuxtemps (1828-1901), whose scores appeared totally at the service of virtuosity as being the maximum expression of the violin's technical possibilities.

The second half of the 19th century is a period historically associated with great political and social change and with the affirmation and the growth of the principles of nationalism. And so this period gave birth to the "nationalist" musical schools. The third group of composers to write concertos for violin is constituted of exponents of these schools: Pyotr Il'yich Tchaikovsky (1840-1893), Antonin Dvorak (1841-1904), Robert Schumann (1810-1856), Edouard Lalo (1823-1892), Joseph Joachim (1831-1907), Johannes Brahms (1833-1897) Max Bruch (1834-1920), Camille Saint Saens (1835-1921), each inspired by the musical culture of his respective homeland.

For example the strong national character of Tchaikovsky's 1878 concerto, one of the first Russian concertos for violin, is a consequence not only of the presence of a traditional Russian dance (called the Trepak) as the third movement but also of the presence of themes and melodies from popular folk tradition. Tchaikovsky dedicated the concerto to Leopold Auer, one of the 19th century's major violin instructors. The practice of dedicating a violin concerto to a particular performer would become a widespread custom through the course of the 1900's. This is a subject that will be elaborated on later.

Written in the same year, 1878, Johaness Brahms' concerto for violin in D major op. 77 is among the most representative concertos of the Romantic period. In three movements, dedicated to Joseph Joachim, it was defined by Wieniawski "unplayable" and Pablo de Sarasate refused to perform it. The score for the solo instrument is technically complex and provides for the frequent use of double strings, rapid scales and arpeggios as well as numerous rhythmic variations.

After having briefly reconstructed the evolution of the concerto for violin and orchestra between the 1700's and 1800's we now want to consider the development and changes the form underwent during the course of the 20th century, presenting the realities of this form that are contemporaneous with the *British* form, this study's primary subject.

The 1900's were, for musical composition, a period of intense linguistic, stylistic and formal change, both in symphonic and instrumental compositions.

One of the first violin concertos of the 20th century is the neo-Romantic Concerto in D minor op. 47 by Jean Sibelius (1865-1957), composed in 1903 and revised in 1905. Virtuosity and melodies evoking a northern atmosphere intertwine: "in an important orchestral score and dazzling soloistic part."[2] In the first movement, an *Allegro* in sonata form, the development section was substituted by an extended cadenza that begins above a timpani roll, in place of the classic use of arpeggios that was characteristic of 18th century concertos.

---

[2] J.Herbage The Concerto, Ralph Hill

The second movement, an adagio in the form of a romanza opens with the orchestra, which introduces a *cantabile* and dramatic violin melody, accompanied in the first part by dissonant brass.

The last movement, in rondò form, is structured on a theme from the clear rhythmic design announced by the timpani and the low strings, which the soloist develops while displaying his virtuosity, with variations on double strings, split octaves, harmonics and trills.

Other concertos that we can define as neo-Romantic are: the Concerto in A minor, op. 82 (1904) by Alexander Glazunov (1865-1932), notable for its dazzling style and its organization in a unitary structure that connects the three movements and the cadenza; the Concerto, op. 33 by the Dane Carl Nielsen (1865-1931), written in 1911; and Erich Wolfgang Korngold's (1897-1957) Concerto in D major, op. 35, composed in 1945, dedicated to Alma Mahler and performed for the first time in 1947 by Jascha Heifetz.

The neo-Romantic Concerto in A major, op. 101 by Max Reger (1873-1915) was composed in 1908. With "his strongly chromatic language, [Reger] significantly pushed the limits of tonality." The piece influenced the composer Arnold Schoenberg (1874-1951) and the Second Viennese School, which developed in Vienna between 1903 and 1925 and was constituted of a group of composers led by Schoenberg and his students Anton Webern (1883-1945) and Alban Berg (1885-1935). Leaving behind a post-Romantic compositional style for atonal, chromatic expressionism, the Second Viennese School came to the serial, dodecaphonic technique of Schoenberg. The Violin Concerto, op. 36 by Schoenberg (1936), was written in America during his "voluntary exile" from Nazi Germany. Schoenberg wrote of his work: "I am pleased to add another 'unplayable' work to the repertoire." The concerto, in which the dodecaphonic technique is applied, is in the traditional 3 movement form. The part for violin is extremely complex, to the extent that a celebrated violinist of the day said to the composer "To perform it you will have to wait for a violinist who has 6 fingers." Schoenberg answered "I cannot wait." And so the first performance of the concerto took place December 6th, 1940, with Louis Krasner playing violin and with the Philadelphia Orchestra, conducted by Leopold Stokowski, accompanying. Louis Krasner was the violinist who commissioned Alban Berg's Concerto for Violin and Orchestra in 1935.

In those years Berg was working on his *Lulu* and suffered the death of an intimate friend, Mano Gropius (Alma Mahler's and Walter Gropius's daughter). The event convinced him to work on the concerto, giving it the character of a Requiem and dedicating it to "The memory of an angel."

The concerto is constituted of 2 parts, each of which is in turn divided into 2 sections, which "form an emotional unity."[3]

The first part, the more static of the two, opens with an Andante *sognante* in sonata form, with an arpeggio of the violin's four open strings, G, D, A, E, followed by an Allegretto, a dance with two trios, the first a waltz and the the second a landler, a traditional Cainthian dance.

The second part, which sharply contrasts with the first, opens with an Allegro "that concludes with a climax that is terrifying in its effect," followed by a calm Adagio based on the chorus "Es ist genung" by J.S. Bach. Berg's score utilizes the dodecaphonic technique and employs, serially, the chromatic scale, favoring a detailed and complex treatment of the orchestral interventions, or in opposition to or sustaining the soloist. Here the soloist experiments with elements of virtuosity such as octaves, harmonics, arpeggios on 4 strings and left-handed pizzicatos.

Igor Stravinsky's Violin Concerto in D major, composed in 1931 for the violinist Samuel Dushkin, is considered one of the greatest examples of the neo-classic style. This style, developed between the two world wars, is characterized by a return to balanced and clearly distinguishable thematic structures that utilize tonality and modality to reproduce the tonal system of the baroque style concerto and the First Viennese School of Mozart and Haydn.

The titles of the movements, Toccata, Ria, Capriccio, all indicate a clear intent on the part of the composer to recover the baroque concerto style. Stravinsky himself underlined the affinity between the finale of his concerto and Bach's Concerto for Two Violins (his favorite violin concerto), in particular "in the soloist's duet with a violin from the orchestra." The orchestration of the concerto is in a chamber, and not symphonic style, as is the case with most of the concertos of the 19th century. No cadenzas are present as virtuosity was not one of Stravinsky's interests, "Virtuosity in and of itself occupies very little of my concerto and I believe the technical difficulty of the piece to be relatively modest."

Composed in Switzerland in 1939 during the composer's exile from Nazi Germany, Paul Hindemith's Concerto for Violin and Orchestra is an expression of anxiety brought about by the outbreak of World War II.

In 1939, in Switzerland, another composer was at work on a violin concerto, Samuel Barber (1910-1981). Barber's Violin Concerto op. 14 is in 3 movements: the first movement, Allegro, opens with a solo violin, *cantabile*, without any accompaniment. The entire movement seems to have a character more akin to a sonata than a concerto. In the second

---

[3] M.Carner The Concerto, Ralph Hill

movement an introduction by a solo oboe gives way to the violin who takes up a rhapsodic theme, followed in turn by the movement's close and the eventual reappearance of the oboe. The Presto in moto finale is the movement of soloistic virtuosity.

Still another piece belonging to the year 1939 is the Violin Concerto in A minor by Ernest Bloch (1880-1959), dedicated to Joseph Szigeti.

In Italy the repertoire for violin was enriched by Ferrucio Buson's (1866-1924) Violin Concerto in D major, op. 35, written in 1899 and Ottorino Respighi's (1879-1936) Gregorian Concerto for Violin and Orchestra in 1921. The structure of the latter is based on the introduction of thematic fragments from the middle ages into violin music.

The 1900's were, for eastern Europe and Russia, a moment for recognizing identity and for working at refining compositional capacity.

The Hungarian Bela Bartok (1881-1945) wrote two concertos for violin. The Concerto No. 1, composed 1907-1908 is dedicated to the violinist Stefi Geyer and was published posthumously in 1956. The concerto is structured in 2 movements, Andante sostenuto and Allegro giocoso. The Concerto No. 2, composed between 1937 and 1938 and dedicated to the Hungarian violinist Zoltan Szekely is based on the verbunkos, a 17th century Hungarian dance and musical genre. The concerto is in three movements: Allegro, Andante, Allegro. The first of these, Allegro non troppo, is in the sonata form in the key of B minor; the second, Andante tranquillo, is in the theme-and-variation form (6 variations) in the key of G major. The last movement, Allegro molto, in sonata and cyclic form, presents variants on the opening movement's material.

The Pole Karol Szymanowski (1882-1937) composed the Violin Concerto No. 1, op. 35 in 1916 and the Violin Concerto op. 61 in 1933. While the Concerto No. 1 was written in his impressionist phase the Concerto No. 2 was inspired by the traditional music of Poland's Tatra region.

Composers like Sergei Prokofiev (1891-1953), Aram Khachaturian (1903-1978), Dmitri Shostakovich (1906-1975) contributed to the creation of a wider violin concerto repertoire in Russia.

Prokofiev's Concerto No. 1 in D major, Op. 19, written between 1916 and 1917 is in three movements (Andantino, Scherzo and Moderato), in cyclic form and utilizes reduced orchestration. The Concerto No. 2 in G minor, Op. 63, composed in 1935, in 3 movements (Allegro, Andante, Allegro) opens with a simple melody, based on traditional Russian music, that is treated in the first two movements. The finale develops a rondo theme that invokes a Hispanic atmosphere. Prokofiev wrote "The number of places in which I wrote this concerto demonstrates the nomadic existence that I am forced to live. The principle theme of the first movement was written in Paris, the second movement's theme was written in Voronezh (Russia), the orchestration was finished in Baku and the concerto's premier took place in Madrid"

Khachaturian, who composed the Violin Concerto in D minor, op. 46 in 1945, wrote: "when in 1940 I began to conceive the concerto my head was full of the sound of Oistrakh's violin," to whom he dedicated the work. The concerto is in three movements (Allegro con fermezza, Andante Sostenuto and Allegro vivace) and is characterized by the employment of elements of Russian character, such as the presence of particular rhythmic patterns and melodic designs that exhibit intense emotional and expressive energy.

Dmitri Shostakovich also dedicated two violin concertos to David Oistrakh. Concerto No. 1 in A minor, op. 77, composed between 1947 and 1948, is in four movements (Nocturne, Scherzo, Passacaglia, Burlesque) with the presence of a cadenza connecting the last two and which calls for an extensive orchestra.

Concerto No. 2 in C# minor, op. 129, written in 1967 as the last of Shostakovich's concertos, is in 3 movements (a Moderato in sonata form, an Adagio subdivided into three parts with a central cadenza and an Allegro finale in rondo form).

However, through time, the form of the concerto for violin and orchestra has been conceived of and defined in different ways. The history of violin scores is today a clear testimony to this continual and complex transformation. Surely it is a transformation determined by factors equally as complex, such as the birth of the modern luthier, the perfecting of instrumental techniques, the spread of certain stylistic and compositional currents, the affirmation of virtuosity and of the figure of the soloist, the diffusion of the public concert and the dedication of a work to a particular performer or composer.

It is hoped that this brief historical account of the violin concerto in the classical, Romantic and modern periods can favor, in the course of this study, the identification of those elements of affinity or resemblance, or to the contrary, of originality and singularity, that characterize and distinguish the violin concertos produced by 20th century British composers from those of their contemporaries.

CHRONOLOGY

A chronology is provided so as to condense and define the temporal sequence of the concertos referred to in this book. Those that here are of primary interest are evidenced in bold:

1844	Mendelssohn
1878	Tchaikovsky, Brahms
1899	**Stanford**, Busoni
1904	Glazunov
1905	Sibelius
1908	Bartok, Reger
1910	**Elgar**
1911	Nielsen
1912	**Coleridge-Taylor**
1916	**Delius**, Szymanowski
1917	Prokofiev
1921	Respighi
1925	**Vaughan Williams**
1930	**Somervell**
1931	Stravinsky
1933	Szymanowski

Chronology

PART I

Introduction

The introduction to the first part of this book proposes, after relating a reflection by an early 20th German thinker, a historical snapshot of music in England between the 1700's and the 1800's, useful for defining the cultural realities of England and the artistic tendencies of the British composers who precede those treated at length in this book.

In 1914 the German writer and thinker Oskar Adolf Hermann Schmitz published, in Monaco, his "Das Land Ohne Music" ("The Land Without Music"), a piece in which he forcefully asserts the artistic and musical incapacity of the English composers and the general incapacity of all of Great Britain, after Henry Purcell, to make significant contributions to European musical culture.

If we want to fully comprehend the conclusions of Schmitz's analysis and the reasons behind the spread of the phrase "land without music," we must sift through certain historical events in Great Britain during the 18th and 19th centuries.

Both the evolution and aesthetic of music in Great Britain during the 18th century were greatly influenced by the presence, for more than 45 years, of the German Georg Friedrich Händel. Händel had arrived in 1710 and "his melodrama *Rinaldo,* performed in London the following year, established Italian opera."[1]

Several scholars suggest that the natural evolution of British music was altered, if not blocked, after the death of Purcell in 1695, by the presence of Händel, "It is pointless to speculate on what would have been the future of English music without the influence of Händel. Certainly the genius of Purcell would not have seen immediate continuation but his music was admired by many and could have produced splendid fruit had it been permitted to develop freely."[2]

Contemporaneous to Händel's Italian melodrama was the Ballad Opera (or semi-opera), which countered, during the first half of the 1700's, as a new comical/theatrical genre composed both of song and dialogue. The

---

[1] Edward Lockspeiser, *Dizionario della Musica e dei Musicisti,* UTET pp.391.
[2] ibidem.

first representative production was the *Beggar's Opera*, using John Gay's libretto and with music inspired by traditional melodies of the day.

The spread and popularity of the ballad operas, the formation of a taste for folkloric elements, with the consequent development of a vast repertoire of songs and glees that were almost exclusively vocal, the absence of national figures able to contribute to the renewal of a musical identity characterized by a strong referral to Purcell, all seem to have determined, from the second half of the 1700's, a gradual decline of classical musical art, operatic or instrumental, in England.

Moreover the presence of numerous foreign musicians, such as Francesco Geminiani and Johan Christian Bach in the 1700's and Muzio Clementi and Felix Mendelssohn in the early 1800's, living on British soil, eclipsed the modest work of a few English composers such as William Shield, Charles Dibdin and William Boyce) rendering them inhabitants of a "land without music."

This period of difficulty, of incapacity, of cultural/musical crisis was gradually overcome beginning in 1837, a year that signaled England's shift towards Victorianism. In this year, the efforts of a number of British composers such as John Field (inventor of the "notturno" as a piano form), William Sterndale Bennet (remembered for his 1843 opera *The Bohemian Girl*) and Arthur Sullivan (author of the famous operettas, the *Savoy Operas*) a new national musical identity slowly began to take shape.

Hubert Parry (active in the field of choral music) and Sir Charles Stanford, whose Concerto for Violin and Orchestra will be analyzed later, were among the protagonists of the English musical renaissance, coming about during the late Victorian years of the 1890's, when "The development of democratic institutions would exercise great influence on musical activity, at first on the social spare and then on the tendencies and style of the composers that had until that period been lacking in original musical creations."[3]

1878 saw the foundation of organizations reminiscent of the 1700's (such as the "People's Concert Society") whose role it was to render classical music accessible to all social classes, faciliting the expansion of music in England up through society's elite. These organizations nevertheless favored the diffusion of those foreign composers on whom the British composers were modeling their own compositions. Among those paying little attention to these tendencies was Sir Edward Elgar, "undoubtedly the composer of this period in which the national spirit was

---

[3] ivi, pp.392.

fully expressed,"[4] who, like Charles Stanford and Frederick Delius, the last of the renaissance generation of composers, will be treated in depth in the following chapters.

The English musical *renaissance*, a term first used in September of 1882 by the Daily Telegraph's Joseph Bennet[5], represented an artistic moment characterized by incredible vigor. It was a moment that, in turn, allowed Great Britain to propose a new national style to the rest of Europe and affirm itself as an active and productive musical reality.

Having briefly related the historical/musical trends in Great Britain during the period between Purcell and Elgar it is now appropriate to consider Schmitz's piece, and in particular the expression "the land without music."

Great Britain endured this cultural and musical crisis during the 18th century because, as we have mentioned, the lack of national composers able to fill the artistic vacuum left by Henry Purcell, the popularity of genres such as the ballad opera, and the presence on British soil of some of the most respected foreign musicians of the era made possible an absence of a national musical style. This trend conspired with a decline in instrumental and operatic music and the emergence of a constant need, particularly pronounced in England, to import the musical models and realities that were developing at the time in Germany, France and Italy.

And so "the land without music" appeared an inappropriate definition for Great Britain later, during the

Victorian period, when composers like Sullivan, Stanford and Parry were able to give life to a new national musical identity and bring about that phase of British music that took on the title "The English Renaissance"

It is true that Schmitz's thesis, which propose that the death of Purcell rendered English music incapable of evolving , was written in 1914 at a time when the "English Renaissance" had not reached full maturity. However we can conclude that Schmitz either ignored or simply did not comprehend the phenomenon. Also the reasons for the use of the expression, "the land without music" seems rooted in an attitude of open anti-English polemic, inspired by strong nationalist sentiment. This was a sentiment adopted by some German critics and scholars who were nevertheless blind to the artistic authenticity of the new British composers.

---

[4] ibidem.
[5] Merion Hughes, *The English Musical Renaissance and the Press 1850-1914: Watchmen of Music*, Ashgate 2002.

This study's treatment of the violin concerto in England between 1900 and 1940, will be preceded by some considerations regarding the last concerto composed in Britain before the turn of the 20th century, Charles Stanford's 1899 concerto.

Charles Villiers Stanford

Born on September 30th, 1852, in Dublin, to John James Stanford (a lawyer and non professional musician), Charles Villiers Stanford began studying violin, piano and organ and was introduced to composition by the most respected Irish musicians of the day (among them Robert Stewart, Joseph Robinson and Michael Quarry).

In 1862 Stanford went to London to study composition under with Arthur O'Leary, under whom he studied

composition. In 1870 Stanford won a fellowship to study at Queen's College of Cambridge, which he would then leave in 1873 for Trinity College (where he was nominated "official organist" and director of the Cambridge University Music Society). Following the advice of the celebrated violinist and composer, Joachim, with whom Stanford had been in contact in 1860 while in Dublin, Stanford went to Germany between 1874 and 1867 to study with Friedrich Kiel. He then returned to London and concluded his academic studies at Oxford, in 1883. That same year he became a professor of composition and of orchestral direction at the Royal College of Music in London (among his pupils there were Frank Bridge, Coleridge-Taylor and Vaughan Williams). From 1888 onward he taught at Cambridge University.

During those years Stanford affirmed his stature as one of the great figures of the renaissance generation of English composers, producing a vast series of choral and orchestral works for various festivals. The two oratorios *The Three Holy Children* (1885) and *Eden* (1891), *Requiem* (1897), *Stabat Mater* (1907) the choral overture *Ave atque vale* (1909), *Songs of the Sea* (1904) and *Songs of the Fleet* (1910) are among some of his notable works.

Of the seven symphonies that he composed between 1876 and 1911, the third, called "Irish,"   found the greatest international success and so assisted in solidifying British musical culture in Europe at the end of the 19th century, The definitive recognition of the artistic value of Stanford's music came about in January of 1899 when, accepting an invitation by the violinist Joachim and pianist Hans von Bulow, the Irish composer attended a concert in Berlin dedicated exclusively to his works. Among those performed were the Festival Overture *Queen of the Seas, Symphony No.4 in F major Op.31* and the *Suite for Violin and Orchestra Op. 32*, written specifically for the event in Berlin and dedicated to Joseph Joachim.

Stanford, "as is made clear by his letters and writings, believed that international recognition was only to be achieved through more universal forms of music such as the symphony, the concerto, the quartet and the opera." [6]Nevertheless it's important to make note of British editors' refusal to publish many of his works that did not fit into category of "large profit and quick returns."[7]

The repertoire that Stanford constructed during his prolific artistic life included the Violin Concerto, treated in the following pages, two piano concertos, part songs, such as *The Bluebird (*1910, using Mary Coleridge's text), music for theater, oratorios, canticles, anthems and theatrical works; "nevertheless in Great Britain his works wouldn't have success, above all because of the deplorable conditions in which they were performed, along with the public's errant conviction concerning the inadequacy of English for musical theater."[8]

A distinctive mark of Stanford's compositional approach, initially influenced by the music of Brahms and Mendelssohn, is the diatonism of harmonic language, in explicit contraposition to Wagnerian chromatism, combined with the lyricism of Irish folk which particularly inspired the composer. His "6 Irish Rhapsodies," composed between 1901 and 1923 is a testament to his affection for Irish folk.

Stanford died on March 29, 1924, in London. His grave in Westminster, which lies next to that of Henry Purcell, represents Great Britain's recognition of his artistic contributions and cultural importance, both as a composer and teacher, in reviving British music. As well, thanks to a new national style, the privileged burial recognizes Stanford's pivotal role in the "renaissance," a period that moved Britain towards a renovated identity, finally able of affirming itself among the various cultural/musical realities of the late 19th century.

Despite his pivotal role in the "English renaissance" Stanford's cultural and artistic output does not appear principally regulated by the composer's desire to push towards something new or original (the modern). Rather it seems that his primary interest was to gradually lead the evolution of a British musical sensibility still tied solely to Purcell towards models consistent with Romanticism and European musical formalism.

---

[6] Jeremy Dibble, *The New Groove of Music and Musicians,* pp.280.
[7] Charles Stanford, "Music and the War" da *Quarterly Review*, 1915.
[8] Judith Blezzard (trad. Roberto Long), *Dizionario della Musica e dei Musicisti UTET*, pp.432.

Harold Samuel, among the first pianists of the 20th century to dedicate himself exclusively to the performance of works by J,S. Bach, remembered Stanford as "the last of the formalists."[9]

"His intolerance of opposing points of view, his prejudices (both political and musical), his cynicism and his refusal to buckle to the pressures of modern music, created tensions among those he taught. Dyson affirmed "in a certain sense the true rebellion (against Stanford) was the most obvious of all the fruits that his method could give."[10]

The rebellion of which George Dyson (British composer born in 1883) spoke refers to that which Otto Karolyi defined as the "second renaissance"[11] or what can be thought of as a new phase of extraordinary productivity for British music set in motion during the final years of the 19th century by Sir Edward Elgar, Frederick Delius, Arnold Bax and John Ireland. This new phase encompassed, during the first half of the 20th century, multiple compositional currents such as "English pastoral," (Cecili Sharp, Ralph Vaughan Williams, Gustav Holst, George Butterworth); the modernists (Arthur Bliss, William Walton, Constant Lambert); the crypto-modernists (Frank Bridge); the Celtic mystics (Rutland Boughton, E. J. Moeran); and finally the musical poetics of Michael Tippet and Benjamin Britten.

A study of some of these composer's violin concertos will allow us to better understand the complexity and multiform character of the British musical reality of the early 1900's, defined by Elgar "an egotism of several"[12]

Violin Concerto in D Major OP.74

Stanford occupied himself with the composing of the Violin Concerto in D Major, Op. 74 in the fall of 1899, dedicating the work "to my friend, E.F.Arbòs," a Spanish violinist and pupil of both Vieuxtemps and Joachim.

The first performance took place on March 7th, 1901 with Arbòs and the Bournemouth Municipal Orchestra, directed by Stanford himself. The work was not received particularly well by critics and Stanford had to wait for performances by the virtuoso Fritz Kreisler, October 7th, 1904 at the Leeds Festival and by the American violinist Achille Rivarde (teacher at the Royal College of Music) in the summer of 1905 at the Philharmonic

---

[9] Jeremy Dibble, *The New Groove of Music and Musicians,* pp.280.
[10] ibidem.
[11] Otto Karolyi, *Modern British Music,* pp.15.
[12] From Michael White, "So Mighty, So Unmusical: How Britannia Found Its Voice", *The New York Times*, February 2007.

Society before he could witness full appreciation of his work's artistic value.

Considered by Hubert Parry, a composer belonging to the generation of the English renaissance, to be one of Stanford's most significant works, the concerto "was unable to get itself into the canon of the most popular violin concertos"[13] and the full score, after Stanford's death, was not published for 10 years, rendering it "virtually unknown"[14]. In 2004 Breitkopf and Härtel published an adaptation for violin and piano.

First movement, *Allegro:* the fineness of the winds' figurations and of the strings' pizzicatos, which both characterize the refined and soft orchestral tessitura of the exposition's opening measures and introduce the soloist's theme (first played in the key of D major and then immediately presented in minor) brings about the first *tutti*, modulating to the relative minor key of B. "Stanford seems to strongly prefer the Mendelssohnian form of the "divided" sonata scheme rather than the more classic fusion of ritornello and sonata typical of Brahms[15]. A lyrical revival of the solo follows, one in which a fragment in 3/2 time is played only on the 4th string, interposed with various *tutti* passages..

The development section opens with an energetic tutti of 60 measures (keeping with the classical tradition). It is followed by an episode of extended lyricism by the soloist that will again bring about an orchestral recapitulation where a new presentation of the principle theme of the exposition alternates with soloistic sections of great technical complexity, between lyricism and virtuosity. This moves towards a finale, in *crescendo*, of octaves and double-stopped chords, which then concludes with a perfect cadence n the movement's original key.

Second movement, *Canzona – Andante*: in the form of a three part *canzone*, the second movement opens with the exposition by the clarinets and trombones of a descending pattern, in G minor, of 6 notes, on which Stanford based the material of the entire movement.

Here the solo part characterized by great melodic intensity. In the first section this is expressed by the dark timbres of the G string.

The central section presents, moving to the key of E flat major, the diatonic approach typical of Stanford's compositional practice. The last section of the movement, in returning to the opening key of G minor, has

---

[13] Jeremy Dibble, *The Romantic Violin Concerto 2,* booklet CD. Hyperion 2000.
[14] ibidem.
[15] ibidem.

the soloist performing a cadenza, which is then followed by a conclusion of dreaming G major arpeggios.

Third movement, *Allegro Moderato*: a moment of the maximum expression of the technical possibilities of the violin, the third movement sees the orchestra and soloist dedicated to revisiting, in a movement constantly modulating between the keys of D major and B minor, a rondo theme. The atmosphere of a traditional dance was suggested by Stanford himself with his direction on the score: "Gaelic air."

Stanford's score appears heavily inspired by the great violin concertos in D major by Beethoven, Brahms and Tchaikovsky. The key of D major is a common choice by composers who are aware of the possibilities for extreme virtuosity and technical brilliance that the key offers the performer.

The Concerto for Violin and Orchestra, Op. 61 by Ludwig van Beethoven (1806) saw its definitive affirmation within the wide repertoire of violin concertos only in the 1840's, thanks to the work of philological and musicological recovery carried out by Mendelssohn and the performances of Joseph Joachim, long held to be the best interpreter of Beethoven's piece.

Stanford, who we remember as being strongly tied to the German violinist, seems in his concerto to want to renew that elegant majesty of Beethoven's work, distinguished by the absolute balance between lyricism and virtuosity. Particular melodic patterns, such as that of the last two measures of the first movement's finale seem to be true and are references to prop references to Beethoven's concerto.

Johannes Brahms dedicated his 1878 work, the Concerto for Violin and Orchestra in D major, Op. 77, to Joseph Joachim who advised the composer in the scoring of the soloistic part and so determined some of the strictly technical performative aspects; later we will have the opportunity to consider, in greater depth, this phenomenon of the cooperation between composer and performer that was so widespread in the 1900's.

The concerto, beyond exemplifying a high level of technical complexity, appears determined by a desire to strike a balance between lyricism, virtuosity and symphonic character, a quality exhibited by the work of Beethoven who Stanford, so near to Brahms' Romantic feeling, wanted to emulate.

In the initial historical compendium we already touched briefly on the Concerto for Violin and Orchestra in D Major, Op. 35 by Pyotre Ilyich

Tchaikovsky. Here it is appropriate to remember that, like Brahms, Tchaikovsky also received suggestions for technical performative aspects in the soloistic score from a violinist, Yosif Kotek (the concerto was dedicated to the violinist and instructor Lepold Auer).

The four concertos turned out structurally similar: an extended first movement, *Allegro*, in the cases of Beethoven and Brahms also of significant symphonic character; a second movement of expansive lyricism, in *canzone* form in the cases of Stanford and Tchaikovsky whose works, along with Brahms', open with an introduction by solo woodwinds; a third movement, *danza,* in rondo form, that sees the presence of folklore elements: Hungarian in the case of Brahms, Russian in Tchaikovsky and Scottish in Stanford.

Stanford's work seems to want to tend towards a formal synthesis of "old" and "new" in the unification of elements of the compositional poetics of classicism and elements of musical Romantic feeling, "one of the most fascinating aspects of this 'interaction' is the way which the composer permits one to influence the other, at the same time being sure that the 'new' never gets the upper hand."[16] All this confirms Stanford's artistic capacity for reinventing British music, with an eye towards the compositional parameters of the 19th century European musical tradition, while at the same time seeking to negate the non-academic expressions of it (as his position was one of severe anti-modernism).

It is hoped that this brief reflection on the 19th century's last concerto for violin and orchestra, in England, can move us towards a more complete comprehension of the mutations and transformations that this genre underwent during the course of the 1900's, a path that we will trace through a study of the very "new" that Stanford so feared would seize the upperhand.

Edward Elgar

Among the principle agents of British music's development at the beginning of the 20th century (a phase defined as the "Second Renaissance") is undoubtedly Edward Elgar who "alone was able to restore the desert of 19th Romantic period in 19th century England, devoting himself to creating respect for 'national' music"[17].

---

[16] ibidem.
[17] Otto Karolyi, *Modern British Music,* pp.15.

Born in Broadheath, a small village of Worcestershire country, on June 2nd, 1857, to William Henry Elgar and Ann Greening, Edward was the fourth of 7 children.

His father, an organist, pianist and violinist opened a music shop in Worcester, in 1863, where Elgar passed his infancy undergoing an autodidactical musical education and receiving violin lessons, initially from a local instructor and then in London, between 1877-88, under Adolf Pollitzer, director of the New Philharmonic and Royal Choral Society.

In 1872 he left school to work in a local lawyer's firm, only to then dedicate himself, from 1873 on, exclusively to music, becoming the organist of Worcester's St. George's Roman Catholic Church (1885-9), director of the Worcester Amateur Instrumental Society (1877) and the Worcester Philharmonic (1877), band master of the County Lunatic Asylum of Powick (1879-1884), orchestral violinist in the Worcester and Birmingham music festivals (in 1844 directed by Dvorak) and a violin and piano teacher. In 1889 he married his piano student, the writer Caroline Alice Roberts, daughter of Major Henry Gee Roberts.

From 1890 Elgar composed continually, beginning with the scoring of *Froissart*, overture for orchestra, Op. 19, the *Serenata for String Orchestra,* Op. 20 (1892), the symphonic cantata *The Black Knight* for choir and orchestra, Op. 25 (1892), *Three Bavarian Dances* for orchestra, Op. 27 (1897).

Elgar's full affirmation as a national composer, authentic innovator and anti-academic reformer of British music came about in London, on June 19th of 1899 with Hans Richter's direction of the first performance of the *Variations on an Original Theme "Enigma"* for orchestra, Op. 36.

The *Enigma Variations,* which "lose that stale and academic flavor that had marked the classic variations on the given theme,"[18] is composed of 14 brief variations that portray, with music, 14 different individuals who were close to the composer as well as present an original score characterized by variety in terms of its melodic, rhythmic and harmonic patterns. The piece departs from stylistic formalism and is particularly attentive to orchestral tessitura and color as well as to possible timbric combinations. The piece seeks out an intense sound/style that is charged with expression and the "British feeling" that is distinctive of Elgar's national poetics.

On the occasion of the 1900 Birmingham Festival Elgar composed the oratorio *The Dream of Gerontius* Op. 38 "in which he expressed his Catholic faith in the form of a strange union between the tradition of the

---

[18] Edward Neill, *Dizionario della Musica e dei Musicisti UTET,* pp.641.

Haendelian oratorio and some aspects of Wagnerian musical thought."[19] Based on the namesake text by cardinal Newman, the oratorio was presented for the first time on October 3rd, 1900, under the direction of Hans Richter. Initially it did not receive a positive critical reception.

However the oratorio obtained wide and definitive acclaim after its second performance, on December 19th, 1901, in Dusseldorf. The success renewed interest in British music, which was now able to engage audiences as an expression of the nation's artistic identity.

Elgar, defined by Richard Strauss as "the first English progressist composer" assumed the role of principle promoter for this new "patriotic" music. Elgar's idea was a music far from Stanford's academicism, not regulated by pre-established models (and so imitative). His conception was of a music that represented the free and authentic expression, albeit moderate, of Great Britain's modern artistic sensibility.

During the first decade of the 1900's Elgar worked extensively on the scoring of symphonic works like the *Cockaigne Overture*, Op. 40 (1901), *Introduction and Allegro*, Op.47 (1905), the *Symphony No.1 in A flat Major*, Op.55 (1907-8), the *Symphony No.2 in E flat Major*, Op.63 (1909-1911), the *Concerto per Violino e Orchestra*, Op.61 (1910, that we will treat shortly, Pomp and Circumstances Marches, Op.39 (1901-1930). The Concerto for Cello and Orchestra in E Minor Op.85 (1918-1919), in an evident stylistic transformation coming about as a result of a painful period endured by the composer during the war years, is the epoch's conclusive work, "The Romanticism of the late Victorian period and the Eduardian period, so my dear Elgar, is finished"[20].

After the death of his wife in 1920, "with whom a creative part of Elgar died" [21] the composer dedicated himself to the realization of some of the first recordings of his work. Between 1932 and 1934 he continued to work, with difficulty due to a malignant tumor, at the scoring of a third symphony. The piece remained unfinished.

Elgar passed the better part of his life outside the city. His tie with the countryside, and with nature in general, brought him back to a quest for purity. It is that spontaneity, authenticity, inspired by his contact with nature that is so characteristic of his compositions: "There is music in the air, music all around us, the world is full of it and you simply take as much as you require."

---

[19] Otto Karolyi, *Modern British Music,* pp.16.
[20] ivi, pp.17.
[21] Diana McVeagh, *The New Groove of Music and Musicians,* pp.121.

His education as a youth, as we've noted, was entirely autodidactic and, in this sense, his distance from the city meant distance from the academic sensibility of the "official" musical institutions of the day. Elgar's approach was indeed different from the artful formalism of some of his contemporaries (like Stanford). Elgar attempted to translate into music authentic British feeling and combine it with the musical ideal of the German Romantic tradition.

"There are many possible futures [for English music]. But the one I want to see coming into being is something that shall grow out of our own soil, something broad, noble, chivalrous, healthy and above all, an out-of-door sort of spirit"[22].These are Elgar's words spoken in March, 1905 at the University of Birmingham, encouraging his music students towards the discovery of an authentic, new creativity, capable of ensuring Great Britain a bright musical future.

The composer, who worked to open up new expressive and compositional possibilities seemed to want to move towards significant change; nevertheless he was still fascinated by the last propositions of Romantic culture. Elgar will never be considered part of the Modern movement of 20th century British composers. Instead he remains within that "egotism of several," an elegant and capable mediator of "old" and "new."

In concluding this biographical sketch it appears appropriate to draw a brief comparison of the two coeval composers that we have treated so far: Stanford, from Ireland, formally educated, tied to the musical institutions of the day and Elgar, the English autodidact, whose education occurred mostly outside of those institutions.

The two composers united in the stylistic choice of mediating "old" and "new," both revolting against the Romantic tradition and opposing the supremacy of Modernity, diverged with respect to the reasons of their actions and in their musical thought.

Putting aside the technical and formal differences of the works, which we will discuss at length during an analysis of Elgar's Violin Concerto, here we can compare the composers' respective attitudes: drawing on his academic experience and in the spirit of imitation of the formal, dominant models of classicism and Romanticism, Stanford seemed to want to reorder and restructure British music towards a total adherence to the principles of 19th century European musical culture; Elgar, though strongly influenced by the German romantic tradition, appears to have been mostly

---

[22] *A Future for English Music and other Lectures*. By Edward Elgar. Ed. by. Percy M. Young. Dobson London 1968.

involved in seeking out "something that shall grow out of our own soil," with the objective being the expression of "national feeling." And in the case of Elgar his means were exclusively his, original and not inspired by an external musical culture.

The coexistence of two attitudes that represented such disparate sensibilities reveals the gradual tendency in British musical culture, at the turn of the century, to acquire a composite and multiform character. It was this character that ushered in the possibility for the peaceful cohabitation of multiple compositional currents during the 20th century.

Concerto for Violin and Orchestra in B Minor OP.61

"I wish Elgar would write something for the violin....it would be certainly effective"[23]. With these words, spoken during an interview with the Hereford Times in 1905, the violinist Fritz Kreisler inspired the British composer Elgar to write a violin concerto.

In 1906 Elgar received the Austrian virtuoso's request though he would only go to work on the composition of the concerto in 1909 when he received the official commission from the Royal Philharmonic Society.

The score, originally conceived in Hereford (where the composer was living with his wife), continued to be sketched out in Italy (during a sojourn in 1909) only to then be finalized in London between June and July of 1910.

Despite direct knowledge of the violinistic idiom in May of 1910 Elgar turned to the musician W.H. Reed, first violinist of the London Symphony Orchestra, for suggestions regarding the writing of the solistic section of the concerto (in its more technical dimensions). Elgar would also invite Reed to a private performance, in September, at the house of Herbert Brewer, in Gloucester. [24]

The first public performance took place with Elgar directing on November 10th, in 1910, at the Queen's Hall of London. Fritz Kreisler was the soloist. The score of the concerto, dedicated to Kreisler, was published with the Spanish caption: "Aquì està encerrada el alma de....." (Herein is enshrined the soul of ...) a quote from the picaresque novel *Gil Blas* by the French author Alain-Renè Lesage.

---

[23] Fritz Kreisler, *Hereford Times,* 7 October 1905.
[24] W.H.Reed, *Music & Letters, Vol.16*, No.1 (Jan.,1935), pp.36.

The quote is widely held as referring to Alice Stuar-Wortley (daughter of the English painter John Evertt Millais), an intimate friend of Elgar and generally believed to be the primary source of inspiration for the work.[25]

First movement, *Allegro*

The *Allegro*, in sonata form, begins with a large orchestral exposition of symphonic character that is, in a typically classical fashion, articulated over 2 sections: a first section spanning measures 1-30 and a second section spanning measures 31-69.

4 different themes are present in the first section, that Herbert Byard argues should be considered "phrases" given their brevity.[26]

theme (a)

theme (b)

The melodic line of theme (a), twice played by the first violins, moves in the fifth measure of theme (b), which repeats itself a second time, in the seventh measure, in a syncopate pattern.

Theme (c), which is 10 measures long and recurs 3 times with different orchestration and in different keys leads to theme (d), which unfolds in 12 measures. Theme (d) concludes the first section of the orchestral exposition.

---

[25] The Elgar Society and The Elgar Foundation website http://www.elgar.org/.
[26] Herbert Byard, *Edward Elgar from The Concerto,* Ralph Hill.

theme (e)

theme (f)

The second section, which exhibits a more modulating character, is constituted of a theme (e), a *cantabile* played by the strings, This theme is tied to theme (f), which is a harmonic variation of theme (b)'s melodic line. The development of theme (f) moves, in an intense climax of strings and winds, towards a new affirmation of theme (a), with follows, *nobilmente*, the entrance of the solo violin who concludes the long orchestral exposition.

Elgar reworked the classic *tutti* beginning by employing short thematic phrases kept close to one another by the melody's continual flow. This melody is distributed through the entire orchestra and seeks out the timbric variety that is distinctive of the score.

The soloist, after a brief *recitativo,* "in which it completely dominates the scene as if a great philosopher had suddenly decided to clarify the questions raised during an animated discussion in which his students had just intervened"[27] It presents a new exposition of theme (b), *cantabilie* and *largamente,* now developed in an elaborated rhythmic and heavily modulating writing.

A lyrical variation of theme (e), in the key of G major, follows and concludes with a transitory orchestral recapitulation of theme (a). This anticipates a new intervention by the soloist, in the key of F # minor. It is a moment of virtuosistic re-elaboration (chords, split octaves, descending chromatic scales) of themes (c) and (e).

The solo's climax resolves in a *tutti* that picks up theme (d), *con passione,* then *maestoso*, a return to theme (e), an episode of strong modulation that is followed by theme (a), first with the orchestra and then

---

[27] Herbert Byard, *Edward Elgar from The Concerto*, Ralph Hill.

with a new intervention by the soloist, in recitavo, accompanied by 4
muted horns who echo the rhythmic design of theme (d).

The final coda, introduced by the orchestra with theme (b) in the
syncopated version, played *con fuoco,* concludes the first movement. The
coda features solo passages, arpeggios and chords played on double
strings, all in the key of B minor, in perfect cadenza.

Second movement. *Andante*

The *Andante* in the key of B flat Major is a moment of intense
lyricism. It opens with an exposition of theme (a), on strings, accompanied
by woodwinds and horns. The eighth measure of the theme sees theme (b),
played by the solo violin, serve as a counterpoint.

theme (a)

theme (b)

After a brief dialogue, the soloist and orchestra move with theme (c)'s
modulating pattern towards a new tonal region, D flat major, that will see
its full declaration with theme (d).

theme (c)

theme (d)

The episode in D flat major concludes with the orchestra's playing of theme (c), in the key D major, and the violin's introducing of theme (e).

The orchestra and soloist follow by elaborately reproposing the principle themes (a) and (b), a definitive return to the original key of B flat major. The final coda opens with theme (c), now in a different key, seeing the re-exposition of the preceding episode's melodic patterns (in D flat major) which echoes back to the strings' playing of theme (d).

Third movement. *Allegro Molto*

The strings introduce the soloist's nervous quintuplets (in crescendo) with 4 quatrains of semiquavers. This is followed by a section "in which the solo violin seems to be playing a kind of prelude on a figure of rising turns"[28]; clarinets, bassoons and violas foreshadow, in measures 20-21, the theme (b).

The exposition of theme (a), in the key of D major, takes place with a *tutti* in *fortissimo*. This is followed by the soloist's entrance. The exposition is concluded by the full enunciation of theme (b).

theme (a)

theme (b)

New melodic and rhythmic designs, theme (c), now combine with theme (b), moving towards a brief lyric episode in B major, theme (d), that echoes the atmosphere of the second movement.

---

[28] Donald Francis Tovey, *Essays in Music Analysis Vol. III Concertos.*

theme (c)

theme (d)

Initial quintuplets, played by the solo violin, begin the re-exposition of themes (b), (c), and (d) and the presentation of a new lyrical moment, cantabile (*Nobilmente*), inspired by the second movement's (c). The coda dissolves with a canon of theme (b) in diminuendo.

A *Cadenza accompagnata* follows in which strings evoke the first movement's theme (a). Here the strings are divided into two groups: the first muted and the second group tremolando on the bridge and "pizzicato tremolando." Here the composer seems to have wanted to establish great flexibility in how the solo score will be interpreted – arpeggios that are rhythmically varied, chords of thirds, fourths, fifths, sixths, chromaticism – seeking out a "cantabile" and expressive kind of virtuosity, distant from just technical ostentation.

The orchestra and soloist's final, distinct affirmation of the first movement's theme (a) concludes the *cadenza*.

The final coda, begun with the initial introduction of the *Allegro Molto*, sees the second movement's melodic theme (c) re-evoked by the strings who align themselves alongside the solo violin's brilliant and virtuosistic figures. After raising itself up on ascending triplets of sixths, sustained by a noble crescendo of horns, the violin and orchestra conclude in a perfect cadenza, in the bright key of B major.

> "... a new life is born within an old form that was in danger of decaying, across which everywhere the author's personality is expressed. Now Elgar has a style, a personal idiom, that none of them who know his work can confound in the mass."[29]

Ernest Newman, *Elgar's Violin Concerto The Musical Times*, Vol.51, No.812

So Ernest Newman would comment on Sir Edward Elgar's Concerto for Violin and Orchestra in October of 1910, one month before the concerto's public performance in London.

In wanting to fully comprehend the meaning of Newman's reflection we must adequately define those distinct elements of the "new life," the elgarian writing present in the work here treated.

The English composer based his concerto on the structural model of the "old form," the classical form, characterized by division into 3 movements: Allegro, Andante, Allegro. In moving away from the tradition, with the absence of cadenzas in the first 2 movements, he presents the only episode of *Cadenza accompagnata* in the last movement, as a true and authentic technical innovation.

The extended, initial orchestral exposition demonstrates itself to is an element of continuity with violin concertos of the 19th century, as in the cases of Beethoven and Brahms. Nevertheless the principle with which the English composer introduced the soloist appears absolutely innovative; the entrance of the solo violin completes the exposition of theme (a), begun by the orchestra 2 measures earlier. Reed (the violinist to whom the composer would turn for advice regarding the technical-performative aspect of the concerto) remembers Elgar's enthusiasm concerning the entrance of the soloist "with the concluding half of the principal subject instead of at the beginning."[30]

The first movement's thematic material, as our analysis suggests, is not arranged according to the 19th century repartitioning into first and second subject. On the contrary 6 different thematic fragments are presented in a continual flow of melody so as to "generate that ecstatic sense of an inevitable and harmonious evolution, as with that of an organic whole."[31]

The symphonic character of the initial *Allegro* is never heavy or harsh but rather intensely dynamic and vibrant both in sound and orchestral tessitura. It is an expression of a vital and vigorous solemnity. The orchestral instrumentation (strings, 2 flutes, 2 oboes, 2 clarinets, 2 bassoons, a double bassoon *ad libitum*, 4 horns, 2 trombones, 3 trumpets, a tuba *ad libitum* and timpani) confirms the composer's decision to seek out new timbres that would serve the fluid deconstruction of the melodic line, towards a continual dialectic between the different instrumental identities of the orchestra.

(Oct.1,1910) pp.631.
[30] Phillip Huscher, *Chicago Symphony Orchestra Program Notes.*
[31] ibidem.

The solo violin itself engages in a harmonious dialogue with the orchestra in a uniform exchange of thematic phrases and rhythmic designs, contributing to the conversion of the roles of single accompaniment (by the orchestra) typical of the "old form," towards a more complex and "modern" combination of *tutti* and solo. The strong Romantic lyricism of the Elgarian solo score, conceived *nobilmente*, seems to determine an expressive use of technical virtuosity. It is not just a moment of brilliant and rhapsodic violinistic performance but rather a means to bring about the composer's more intimate and profound melodic/musical thoughts.

The second movement, *Andante*, is the moment in which the concerto's lyrical character is fully affirmed, The melodic line of the solo violin, often in counterpoint with the orchestra, is arranged in intensely strong passages, played on the fourth string only, and in ecstatic and dreamy phrases in the instrument's higher registers, sometimes united in a sought after arabesque. In this way the composer determined a single lyricism of 2 different temperaments: an impassioned, ardent one and a fluid, serene one. Together they represent the emotional complexity of Elgarian musical feeling.

In the final movement, *Allegro Molto*, the energetic and passionate character of the instrumental virtuosity is fully realized. This is accomplished by the employment of an advanced violinistic technique (chromaticism, chords, octaves harmonic), which complements a score that is adorned with complex rhythmic and harmonic lines.

The most evident structural innovation is the presence of the *Cadenza accompagnata*, "an interlude of serious and profound contemplation, as it were the soul retiring into itself and seeking its strength inwardly, in the midst of the swirling life all round it"[32]

The effect *pizzicato tremolando*, that according to the composer's markings on the score "should be "thrummed" with the soft part of three or four fingers across the strings," echoes the sound of "distant Aeolian harps murmuring above and below the solo violin."[33]

The *Cadenza*'s closing, with a new exposition of the first movement's opening theme in *lento espressivo nobilmente*, reveals an organic conception of the concerto form that is nevertheless non-circular. Elgar's concerto seems to represent the evolutionary trajectory of that "organic whole" that is a main feature of Elgarian musical thought. This is to say that the melodic line and harmonic unity of the different thematic ideas are never drastically divided into single, autonomous/independent episodes.

---

[32] ivi, pp.634.
[33] ibidem.

Each of the orchestra's individual instruments participates with the soloist in the melody's exposition, the fabric of which, in reality, is composed of closely aligned, individual thematic cells that appear unitary and indivisible.

The same articulated harmonic line, begun in the key of B minor and concluded in B major, seems to signify, in the concerto's finale, the composer's emotional rebirth, both as a personal change and a conclusion of a long, interior voyage. It is hoped that that now we can not only comprehend but also agree with Newman's reflection concerning "..a new life is born within an old form that was in danger of decaying..". The Elgarian compositional poetic, earlier defined as a synthesis of "old" and "new," finds its full application in the Violin Concerto, whose "old form" in 3 movements is cast in a "new" light by those elements that are totally original.

Sir Elgar would set the basis for the creation of a new, compositional approach to the violin concerto form in England. This new approach saw the expression of a musical feeling that was different from the late Romantic period and was inspired by a modern artistic ideal that would bring innovation to composition.

Kreisler, Ysaye, Menuhin

Dedicating a solo concerto to a specific performer was a common practice for 19th century composers. The period saw the advent of both a renewed professional category of instrumentalists and those virtuosos whose primary function was the public performance of their instrument's solo repertoire. The custom, coupled with the way in which a performer might himself commission a concerto from a composer, saw its full affirmation in the 20th century.

Fritz Kreisler would confide, in a 1909 interview: "Sir Edward Elgar promised me a concerto three years ago. When he writes one it will be a labour of love rather than profit." And with these words the concerto's commission was made public.

Fritz Kreisler, born February 2nd, 1875, in Vienna, was one of the greatest violin virtuosos of his day. It was his father who'd introduced him to the violin, though he'd go on to refine his skill at the Conservatory of Vienna, with J. Auber and Hellemesberger and then, in 1885, with Massart and Delibes. At the age of 13 he debuted at New York's Steinway Hall. In

1888 he was denied admittance to the Wiener Philharmonic Orchestra and so decided to study medicine and painting. International recognition of his absolute talent came the following year, with a memorable performance at the Vienna Philharmonic.

Throughout life Kreisler would performance frequently and also pursues the study of composition and the critical study of the principal violin concertos. He died in New York on January 29, 1962.

The Austrian violinist and English composer, both at the forefront of the European musical scene, were first in contact in 1905. The reasons that brought Kreisler to commission the concerto from the "first progressist English musician" were multifold, as were the reasons for which Elgar accepted the proposal.

Mutual admiration was probably only part of the reason why the two were drawn to each other. In fact it would be reasonable to suggest that the desire for recognition and notoriety were among the primary factors to motivate the collaboration. In availing himself to one of the greatest virtuosos of the time, Elgar saw the possibility of consolidating his success in an international context (and so bringing British music to a wider European audience). In turn Kreisler saw the opportunity to become the first performer of a violin concerto produced by one of music's major figures (at the time).

As he was aware of the composer's preparation and knowledge of the violin's technical possibilities, Kreisler did not contribute to the scoring of the concerto (this was a departure from common practice). Nevertheless, as we have already made note, Elgar did collaborate with the violinist W.H. Reed, in 1910. Reed worked on some of the technical/performative aspects of the concerto. The fruit of Kreisler and Elgar's relationship was fully realized with the concerto's first public performance, on November 10th, 1910, at London's Queen's Hall.

Miss Dora Penny, Elgar's friend, remarked of the event: "Kreisler came on looking as white as a sheet, but he played superbly. Edward Elgar was also, obviously, very much strung up, but all went well and the ovation at the end was tremendous. Kreisler and E.E. shook hands for quite a long time…Finally they came in arm-in-arm"[34]

The collaboration continued for successive performances in English concert halls. Due to difficulties organizing with the phonographic recording houses of the day, the concerto, with Kreisler on violin, was never recorded (even if Elgar had anticipated and desired it): "I am to go

---

[34] Michael Kennedy, *Portrait of Elgar,* pp.196.

to Berlin to make records of the Violin Concerto with Kreisler, but it is not quite settled"[35]

Following the collaboration with Kreisler, other gifted virtuosos contacted Sir Edward Elgar: Eugene Ysaye and Yehudi Menuhin. Ysaye performed the concerto, under the composer's direction, solely in Brussels, in March of 1911. Due to a controversy with the editing house Novello, the Belgian violinist would never be able to perform in London.

Yehudi Menuhin was 16 when on July 12, 1932 he first met Sir Edward Elgar. The young American violinist was set to record the concerto (to be released by the recording house HMV) together with Elgar and the London Symphony Orchestra. The recording would take place in London's Abbey Road Studios on July 14th and 15th.

The occasion brought into existence a deep, sincere, mutual admiration between the two. This was to be complemented by a personal affection more akin to that felt between a grandfather and grandson. The experience that the (now elderly) composer had had of his Violin Concerto was regenerated and renewed by Menuhin, a young man full of enthusiasm and vitality, and by the violinist's spontaneous and authentic interpretation of Elgar's work. Elgar wrote to him after a 1932 performance at London's Royal Albert Hall "Your friendship has given me a new zest in life. To hear you play the Concerto gives me the deepest artistic satisfaction... I have never felt such a reading as you gave it, with such thrill of expression"[36]

The definitive recognition of the artistic and personal contribution made by the violinist in performing and popularizing the composer's work came about in May of 1933 when, after the completion of a rehearsal in Paris, the composer added to his score of the Concerto: "Dedicated to Fritz Kreisler and to my dear Yehudi Menuhin."

Their relationship remains one of the most significant testimonies, in 20th century musical history, to true and authentic cooperation between composer and performer and is representative not only of an incredible artistic connection but also a human comprehension. Finally it speaks to an intimate understanding between two extraordinarily complex sensibilities. Listening to their 1932 recording one does not get the impression of there being a 60 year age difference between the two.

The elderly composer, consumed by the impulse and passion of Menuhin's performance, rediscovered the vitality, emotion and youthful brilliance of his score. For Menuhin it was an opportunity to penetrate and

---

[35] ivi, pp.197.
[36] Michael Kennedy, *Portrait of Elgar*.

assimilate a score for which he was now mature enough to comprehend. Thanks also to his exceptional technical skill he could recount the piece to audiences, interpreting it and the complexity of the emotions and sentiments that fed and influenced its creation.

"For me the Elgar concerto will always hold more meaning than a purely musical one, in that it evokes a less universal and more specific atmosphere, one composed of people I love, of places which evoke the roots of my life, a youthful atmosphere of time which must appear to most of us illuminated by nostalgic candlelight compared with the inhuman and merciless glare of contemporary life"[37]

Samuel Coleridge-Taylor

Son of Daniel Peter Taylor, a doctor and native of Sierra Leone, and Alice Hare, a British woman, Samuel Coleridge-Taylor was one of the few non-white British composers. He was born August 15th, 1875 on 15 Theobald's Road, in London's Holborn quarter and introduced to the study of music by Colonel Herbert Walters, an elderly patron and lover of music. At nine Samuel became a member of the St. George's Presbyterian Church and St Mary Magdalene choirs. He received violin lessons from a local teacher, Joseph Beckwith.

In September of 1890, thanks to a friendship between Colonel Waters and Sir George Grove, young Samuel was admitted to the Royal College of Music. Initially he violin and then, from 1892 on, composition with Sir Charles Villiers Stanford who at the time counted among his pupils Vaughan Williams, Frank Bridge, Gustav Holst and William Yeates Hurlstone.

During his education at the Royal College he produced a number of works among which were the *Nonet in F minor for piano, strings and winds* (1894), *Five Fantasiestucke for string quartet* (1895), *Quintet for clarinet and strings* (1895), the *Symphony in A minor* (1896) and the *Quartet for strings in D minor* (1896).

In 1897, with his studies finished, he decided to become a violin teacher at the Croydon Conservatory of Music. Coleridge-Taylor's panafricanist ideology put him into contact with the American poet of colour Paul Laurence Dunbar (1872-1902) whose verse inspired the composer to create *African Romances* op. 17, *Seven Songs for voice and piano*. The following year, on a recommendation from Elgar who saw in

---

[37] Yehudi Menuhin, *Sir Edward Elgar, My musical Grandfather*. Elgar Society 1976.

the young composer "a new English composer of real genius"[38] Coleridge-Taylor received a commission from the Three Choirs Festival, one of the oldest and most prestigious festivals in Great Britain. Coleridge-Taylor used the occasion to compose the *Ballad in A minor*. The work was well received by both the public and critics alike. Edgar himself said "I liked it all and loved some and adored a bit"[39]

The full affirmation of success came for Coleridge-Taylor in November of that year. With Stanford directing the first public performance of *Hiawatha's Wedding Feast* took place at the Royal College of Music. The piece, a cantata for chorus and orchestra, is based on a text by the American poet Henry Wadsworth Longfellow and dedicated to Sir George Grove, "as a slight token of sincerest affection, respect and admiration." Following the *Wedding Feast* were three other cantatas: *The Death of Minnehaha, Overture* and *Hiawatha's Departure,* which eventually substituted *The Song of Hiawatha*, op.30.

In December of 1899, at the age of 24, he married Jessie Walmisley, a well known pianist at the Royal College.

At the beginning of the new century Coleridge-Taylor's music was becoming ever more popular and known, not just in England but also America where, in 1901, the Samuel Coleridge-Taylor Choral Society, an all black choir, was born (in the state of Washington). In 1904 the composer went to the states to direct some of his more recent works (among which were the *African Suite* op. 35 for solo piano and *Toussaint overture* op.46 for orchestra): "Mr. Coleridge-Taylor was the first person of colour to give a concert in Mendelssohn Hall, New York" [40]

Inspired by traditional African folklore, in 1905 Coleridge-Taylor composed the *Twenty Four Negro Melodies*, explaining a program note "What Brahms has done for the Hungarian folk music, Dvorak for the Bohemian, and Grieg for the Norwegian, I have tried to do for these Negro Melodies"[41]. The African-American educator, Booker T. Washing, wrote in the biographical preface to the score "It is especially gratifying that the most cultivated musician of his race, a man of highest aesthetic ideals, should seek to give permanence to the folk-songs of his people by giving them a new interpretation and an added dignity."[42]

---

[38] *Letters to Nimrod.* ed. Percy   M. Young. London 1965.
[39] ibidem.
[40] *The Musical Times*, Vol.50, No.793 Mar. 1909.
[41] *The Musical Times*, Vol.116,No.1590 Aug.1975.
[42]Booker T. Washington, *Twenty Four Negro Melodies* op.59, published in 1905 by Oliver Ditson, Boston.

Coleridge-Taylor, who began teaching composition at the Trinity College of Music in 1903 and then in 1910 both at the Crystal Palace School of Art and Music and the Guildhall School of Music, used those years to develop his skills as a director, becoming the regular director at the Handel Society and the Westmorland Festival. In 1910 Coleridge-Taylor returned to America to participate in the Litchfield Music Festival. The festival's founder, Carl Stoeckel, had been the one to extend the invite (the event prompted the members of an orchestra from New York to give Coleridge-Taylor the nickname "The black Mahler"). The following year the composer dedicated his *A Tale of Old Japan* to Stoeckel who shortly after that commissioned from the composer the *Concerto op. 80,* which will be treated briefly in the coming pages.

On September 1st, 1912, at the age of 37, Samuel Coleridge-Taylor died of pneumonia (aggravated by exhaustion, probably brought on by over-work).

This is a brief synopsis of the life of a composer, didact and British orchestra director. It is a life completely devoted to music, whose language Coleridge-Taylor was able, from a young age, to comprehend and utilize as a means to expression and communication not just of artistic feeling but of the heart and ideas of an entire people, the African people: "As for the prejudice, I am well prepared for it. Surely that which you and many others have lived in for so many years will not quite kill me. I am a great believer in my race, and I never lose an opportunity of letting my white friends here know it. Please don't make any arrangements to wrap me in cotton-wool."[43]

Throughout his life Coleridge-Taylor declared his pride in his heritage, clearly demonstrating, in a number of works, the desire to sustain, promote and spread the traditional, cultural sentiment of the African people. In so doing he was able to use music to courageously oppose the ever growing racist intolerance of the time.

His artistic and compositional intention cannot be translated, as one might expect, in a political/intellectual approach to the creating of music; "He did not thirst for intellectual analysis, for recondite problems, or for odd and self-conscious effects. He wanted to put down what welled up in him quite simply and straightforwardly. Like in half-brothers of primitive race he loved plenty of sound, plenty of colour, simple and definite rhythms, and above all things plenty of tune. Tune pours out in passage

---

[43] Samuel Coleridge Taylor, letter to Andrew Hilyer (14th September, 1904).

after passage, genial and kindly and apt to the subject and, in an emotional way, often warmly and touchingly expressive."[44]

Coleridge-Taylor's compositional poetic, initially akin to Brahms and then closer to Dvorak, beyond utilizing traditional African melodic and rhythmic elements, acquired its distinctive qualities by the employment of varied rhythm. This is felt by the presence an extremely coloured orchestral tessitura that often provides subtle interventions by the brass section and still more by the intense harmonic experimentation that was by that point far from Stanford's Academic teachings.

We hope that this brief treatment, together with an analysis of the *Violin Concerto* op. 80 (that will now be presented) can contribute to rekindling an interest in the "black Mahler" and his artistic work. He is one of the many notable figures that are too frequently forgotten when we think of British music history.

Concerto for Violin and Orchestra in G Minor OP.80

The violin concerto, as has been mentioned, was commissioned in 1911 by Carl Stoeckel who initially brought up the idea of using material derived from African-American spirituals and songs. "Stoeckel had suggested that the projected concerto might incorporate some spirituals and hoped that other American songs, such as "Yankee Doodle" might be used. His wife, Ellen Stoeckel, offered Coleridge-Taylor a spiritual, "Keep Me from Sinking Down" passed on to her by her father."[45]

Conditioned by external influences that significantly limited the stylistic choices available Coleridge-Taylor had to work almost singularly on pre-existing material from folk tradition and so was deprived of the spontaneous, "primitive" character of his work. As was suggested he used "Yankee Doodle" for the final movement and decided finally on the spiritual "Many Thousand Gone" for the second movement (in place of that proposed by Stoeckel's wife).

When the composer submitted the finished work to Stoeckel and Maud Powell, the America violinist to whom the concerto was dedicated, "They were not impressed with it, particularly the finale. The music is sterile and banal, and for this, "Yankee Doodle" is chiefly responsible."[46] Coleridge Taylor decided to rewrite the entire work, excluding the presence of melodies of African-American origin. He then pleaded with Stoeckel to

---

[44] *The Musical Times*, Vol.53, No.836 Oct. 1912.
[45] Geoffrey Self, *Black Music Research Journal*, *Vol.21*, No.2, 2001 pp.278.
[46] ibidem.

destroy the Concerto's first version, which he perceived as the result of an artificial and forced compositional process that had nothing to do with his idea of artistic and musical creation.

The second version was complete in March of 1912. In April the composer thought he had sent the score to America, but it never arrived. It sank, along with the Titanic, the ship whose duty was to bring it across Atlantic. A new copy of the concerto was sent and on June 4th, 1912, the first public performance of the concerto took place at the Norfolk Connecticut Music Festival, with Maud Powell playing violin. "Powell gave her performance under the gaze of a portrait of the absent composer that shared the platform with her and the orchestra."[47]

On the same day the concerto was performed in Croydon, England by violinist W.J. Read. Nevertheless the *official* British premier took place on October 8th, in London's Queen's Hall, with violinist Arthur Catterall and director Sir Henry Wood: "It was five weeks after the composer's death, and if for no other reason it made a great impression. It was heard in the USA, Maud Powell having five dates with it in the following season, including New York and Chicago, but in Europe, where the composer himself had been booked to conduct in Berlin and Dresden, it seems to have been quietly forgotten, apart a performance in Bournemouth in 1913 with a local violinist."[48]

The concerto, which remained unperformed for almost 70 years, finally saw the light of day again in 1980, with Sergiu Schwartz playing violin, on occasion of the centenary of London's Guildhall School of Music and Drama.

First movement, *Allegro Maestoso – Vivace – Allegro Molto*

The first movement opens with an opulent exposition of theme (a), played by the orchestra, that sees in its characteristic element in a rhythmic triplet pattern. It was "the only idea retained from the first version [of the Concerto]."[49] The soloist then enters, accompanied by a new exposition of theme (a) by an orchestra of light and nuanced tessitura. With the conclusion of every thematic phrase the solo violin interjects a sequence of increasingly difficult arpeggios, combining melodic and rhapsodic character.

---

[47] ibidem.
[48] Lewis Foreman, "The Romantic Violin Concerto 5" booklet CD. Hyperion 2005.
[49] Geoffrey Self, *Black Music Research Journal*, *Vol.21*, No.2, 2001.

theme (a)

The soloist introduces, with a rapid scale, a new, rhythmically varied, thematic episode (a1). After a climax the episode is energetically affirmed by an orchestral tutti. A third tutti, founded on the rhythmic and melodic patterns of theme (a) and (a1), is brought about by new elements and thematic variants.

The violin then moves with woodwinds and pizzicatos towards theme (b) *Vivace*. Here the theme, played on the G string, seeks out an intense and penetrating lyricism. The re-emergence of a virtuosistic crescendo by the soloist, and of thematic elements from (a) and (a1) in the orchestra, concludes with a recapitulation of theme (a) in an orchestral tutti. A cadenza, accompanied by rolling timpani on the dominant, follows. The moment recalls Elgar's Violin Concerto with the cadenza accompanied by "thrummed strings." "A cadenza, placed between the first and the second subjects during the recapitulation, was very unusual"[50] The first movement finishes with a 2/4 *Allegro Molto* in which the soloist offers a proud and passionate exposition of theme (a).

Second movement. *Andante semplice – Andantino*

A brief prelude constituted of solo, muted strings opens the *Andante semplice* in 6/8. The solo violin, after presenting a theme of decidedly lyric and melodic character spins "an enchanted reverie with the orchestra"[51]. An energetic tutti signals the passage to a second section in 4/8, *Andantino*, introducing a new theme, then recapitulated by the soloist. The return of thematic elements then concludes "the charming nocturnal slow movement"[52]

---

[50] ivi, pp.279.
[51] Lewis Foreman, "The Romantic Violin Concerto 5" booklet CD. Hyperion 2005.
[52] ibidem.

Third Movement, *Allegro molto-Moderato*

The final movement, in 3/8, is begun by the rhythmic theme (a), which "might be called a free rondo since the outlines of a rondo are present, but Coleridge-Taylor is constantly happy to explore little contrasted vignettes within the music, or follow his rhapsodic inclination where it takes him" [53]

theme (a)

An overwhelming tutti once again presents the majestic, first movement's opening theme. Here it is combined with rhythmic and thematic elements from the second movement and the rondo. The concerto concludes with theme (a) from the first movement, however here it is rhythmically altered "and at the end the opening rhythm is heard once more."[54] The decision to return to the opening rhythm confirms the concerto's cyclical structure.

Even if this brief analysis is somewhat fragmented hopefully it demonstrates that Samuel Coleridge-Taylor's work made substantial contributions to the evolution of the concerto form, in England. It introduced several musical ideas and principles that are particular to Coleridge-Taylor's approach. Among these we can count: the frequent use of repeated themes that are rhythmically and harmonically varied, the particular placement of the cadenza *accompagnata* in the first movement, a brilliant but not ostentatious solistic score, the rhapsodic character of invention, a colourful and diverse scoring.

Despite these qualities the concerto was still founded on Romantic compositional criteria. Both Cesar Franck and Dvorak were known for subdividing their concertos into three movements and adopting cyclic structures. The Concerto for Violin and Orchestra Op. 80 nevertheless exposed the white public to a new and different musical feeling in a time when they had not had contact (in some cases intentionally) with it. "The manner and the style of his talent drew on his ambiguous and difficult origins, without shutting him off from the currents of his time and place.

---

[53] ibidem.
[54] ibidem.

He became, against the odds, part of his culture's tradition, while openly declaring the mixture - foreign and domestic - of elements and ideas which moved him, and it is his ability to flourish in between cultures and to base himself within the junction of different platforms which gives his persona, and his music, the power to speak to our times."[55]

It is therefore held that his creative capacity, able to combine different musical forms and traditions with intimate personal feeling, was the most significant artistic merit possessed by Samuel Coleridge-Taylor, "the first black composer to make an impact on English ears."[56]

Frederick Delius

Frederick Theodore Albert Delius was born on January 29th, 1862 in Bradford (Yorkshire) to a family with German roots. It was said of his father Julis, a wealthy wool merchant, that "although [he] took an interest in music he refused to entertain the idea that the musical profession was fit for a gentleman."[57] The young Delius, first educated at the Bradford Grammar School and then at the International College of Isleworth, nevertheless learned to play the violin at a high level (and also acquired moderate skill on the piano). His desire to make music his profession continued to grow.

Delius was forced to participate in his father's commercial activities, against his will, but saw an opportunity to be independent and in March of 1884 moved to Solana Grove in Florida to cultivate oranges. "You can have no idea of the state of my mind in those days. In Florida, through sitting and gazing at Nature, I gradually learnt the way in which I should eventually find myself, but it was not until years after I had settled at Grez that I really found myself. Nobody could help me. Contemplation, like composition, cannot be taught."[58]

In Florida, in the city of Jacksonville, Delius struck up a relationship with the organist Thomas Ward who would make significant contributions to the youth's musical education, providing him with a sound grasp of theory. The singing of the south's "negro workers," common for the time and place, inspired Delius's first orchestral work, the "Florida Suite."

---

[55] Mike Phillips, Black Europeans for the British Library Online Gallery.
[56] Norman Lebrecht, *Samuel Coleridge-Taylor: One Hit Wonder.* La Scena Musicale Aprile 7 2004.
[57] Ralph Hill, *British Music of our time*, pp.30.
[58] Eric Fenby, *da Fenby on Delius S.Lloyd.* Thames Publishing London 1996.

Delius's progress convinced his father to provide him a proper musical education and Delius was sent to Leipzig Conservatory, in Germany, where he would remain from 1886 to 1888. Here he studied piano under Reinecke and harmony, counterpoint and fugue under Jadassohn. Excessive discipline and academic rigor left a negative mark on Delius's time in Germany however the experience brought him into contact with the Norwegian composer Edvard Grieg, with whom he had developed a bond that continued throughout their lives.

"It was not until I began to attend the harmony and counterpoint classes at the Leipzig Conservatorium that I realized the sterling worth of Ward as a teacher. He was excellent for what I wanted to know and a most charming fellow into the bargain. Had it not been that there were great opportunities for hearing music and talking music, and I met Grieg, my studies at Leipzig were a complete waste of time. As far as my composing was concerned, Ward's counterpoint lessons were the only lessons from which I ever derived any benefit." [59]

In the summer of 1888 Delius moved to Paris where he frequented the principle exponents of the French cultural, artistic and musical scenes (among them Ravel, Faurè, Gauguin, Strindberg, Munch). During his time in Paris he worked on the notable operas *Irmelin* (1890-92), *The Magic Fountain* (1894-5) and *Koanga* (1895-7), on the symphonic poem *Paa Viderne* (1888) and on the orchestral songs *Sajuntala* (1899) and *Maud* (1891). "The eclecticism in these works is evident, his inspiration deriving from the literature of England, Norway, Denmark, Germany and France, medieval romance, North American Indians and Negros, the Florida landscape and the Scandinavian mountainscape."[60]

In 1896 he met the German painter Helen Jelka Rosen with whom he would move to the town of Grez-sur-Loing, near Fontainebleau, the following year. They were married in September, 1903. The first years of the new century marked a notable increase in Delius's artistic output. *A Village Romeo and Juliet* was completed in 1901, the choral work *Sea Drift* in 1904, the mass *A Mass of Life* was written between 1903 and 1905, *Dance Rhapsody* in 1908 and his last opera, *Fennimore and Gerda* was written between 1909 and 1910.

Despite the outbreak of World War I, which forced him to leave Grez-sur-Loing in 1914, the composer continued to produce significantly, among his works were a *Requiem* (1913-1914), the *Violin Sonata* (1915,

---

[59] ibidem.

[60] Martin Lee-Browne, *da Biography for the Delius Society.*

though begun 10 years earlier), a second *Dance Rhapsody* (1916), the *Double Concerto for Violin, Cello and Orchestra* (1915-1916), the *Violin Concerto* (1916, this concerto will be treated in the following pages), *Poem of Life and Love* (1918), and the *Cello Concerto* (1921).

While in Paris, in 1895, Delius had contracted syphilis and by 1924 its consequences proved overwhelming. His career as a composer would conclude due to paralysis accompanied by worsening blindness and mental disturbances. In 1928 Eric Finby, a young English musician and a follower of Delius's work, got word of Delius's condition and transferred to Grez-sur-Loing to assist the composer in scoring his work.

With Finby's help Delius was able to use his final years to conclude some works that had been left unfinished. Among these were *Songs of Farewell* for double chorus and orchestra, *A Song of Summer, Caprice and Elegy* for cello and a small orchestra, *Deux Aquarelles* for strings and a third *Violin Sonata*.

Frederick Delius died on June 10th, 1934 and was buried in Marlotte, near Grez-sur-Loing. In May of 1935 his and his wife's corpse (she died the same year) were brought to Surrey, to the Church of Saint Peters in Limpsfield. "I have often heard people say that Delius was essentially an English composer and expressed the very spirit of the people. Before making such precise statements it is worth remembering that Delius was a true cosmopolitan, which is shown in some of the subjects of his works."[61]

With these words Ralph Hill tried to unite the image of Delius as an *English* composer with that of his being an absolute artist whose music, in drawing inspiration from all humanity, was not restricted to being only an expression of British tradition and culture.

We suggest that the reasons for this musical cosmopolitanism can be traced from his education as a young man, that is from his first experiences with violin and piano in England, to the teachings of Thomas Ward, to his contact with African-American music, to his conservatory education and friendship with Edvard Grieg in Germany, and continuing through his immersion in the French cultural and artistic scene.

The result of such a unique personal and artistic journey is an absolutely original style, characterized by principles of chromatic harmony, by a combination of British post-romanticism with French impressionism and marked by the presence of elements belonging to African-American and northern European musical traditions.

---

[61] Ralph Hill, *British Music of our time*, pp.37.

Frederick Delius, even if far from his homeland (as William Walton later found himself) was able to affirm himself as one of the major English composers of his time. It is hoped that this brief account demonstrates that Delius's reputation was not a result of being "properly English," as many scholars suggest, but rather for his role as an innovator and promoter of a new, complex and heterogeneous compositional poetic.

"Delius's music is perhaps the most difficult of any to write about at length because, comparatively speaking, there is so little variety or contrast in either its mood or its technique. Delius reminds one of a painter like Constable who confines himself to landscape conceived in colours that are restricted to a limited range of half-lights and nuances. In terms of literature one thinks of Thomas Hardy in so far as the characters and their background in his novels are centred around one corner of England. Thus to know and to love one of Delius's most characteristic works is virtually to know and to love all."[62]

Concerto for Violin and Orchestra

In May of 1915, during a concert, Frederick Delius met the English violinist Albert Sammons. Sammons was performing Elgar's Violin Concerto and Delius was impressed by the ability of the "English Kreisler." It didn't take long for Delius to decide to dedicate a concerto to the great performer. The composer was already at work on the Double Concerto for Violin and Cello. With Sammons' help he finished the work between 1915 and 191. The violinist contributed not just in the scoring of the solo part but also to some passages that connected the piece's various movements.

On January 30th, 1919, the work received its first public performance with Albert Sammons on the violin and Adrian Boult directing. The concert, which took place in London, had been organized by the Royal Philharmonic Society.

The concerto is composed of five sections that move without interruption, which we will analyze holding to Christopher Redwood's study in which the piece is described as a single movement in sonata form "Obviously, sonata-form is merely a way of explaining what happens in this work: the music can in no way be said to be *in* sonata-form (in the normal sense) – it is an example of Delius's free yet thematically coherent formal method of evolving a form out an initial idea."[63]

---

[62] Ralph Hill, *British Music of our time*, pp.33.
[63] Christopher Redwood, *A Delius Companion*, pp.259.

With moderate tempo

The first section of the concerto, composed of 93 measures, is presented as a first movement exposition in sonata form, with an initial thematic group, a transition and a second thematic group.

Two measures of orchestral introduction in 4/4 anticipate the violin's entrance with theme (a), six measures in 4/4; the solo score appears rhythmically detailed, in particular in the rhapsodic octave measure "a free variant of (a)"[64]

theme (a)

A three measure passage in ternary tempo, 12/8, follows in which the solo violin expounds theme (b), immediately developed in the two following measures in (b1). In the following three measures, the second of which is in 6/8, the violin presents theme (c).

theme (b)   theme (b1)

theme (c)

A recapitulation of theme (b) is then played by the orchestra. The soloist plays theme (c) in a 4/4 measure and follows with the development of theme (b) for three measures in 12/8. This culminates in an orchestral tutti, once again in 4/4, of the initial theme now in (a1) "a two-bar

---

[64] ivi pp.256.

contraction of it over a dominant seventh on B flat, which acts as an orchestral ritornello (a1)"[65]

theme (a1)

theme (d)

Four measures follow in which the solo violin proceeds with the development of theme (a1), anticipating the following two in 12/8 that will see an exposition of theme (d). A new development of theme (a), in 4/4 time follows. This gives way to a measure in 12/8 that evokes theme (b). This first thematic group concludes at measure 40.

With the transition the soloist plays a new version of theme (d) (that we will call (d1)), in eight 4/4 measures. The last two of these presents the original version of theme (d).

theme (d1)

The solo develops the melodic and rhythmic elements of theme (a) over eight measures in a complex series of bichords and quatrains. In the following three measures, in 12/8, theme (b) re-emerges. It continues until the arrival of an orchestral chorus of theme (a1), which is played over two measures in 4/4. 14 measures in 12/8 follow. Here the violin and orchestra develop theme (d). Two measures of a new tutti in 4/4, playing theme (a1), concludes the transition section.

The second thematic group opens over the following five measures in 4/4 with the contrasting theme (e), presented by brass. The soloist plays split octaves until the arrival of theme (b), played also by the orchestra, in 12/8 measures (the last in 6/8).

---

[65] ivi pp.259.

theme (e)

A tutti orchestra re-expounds theme (e) in three 4/4 measures. Five 4/4 measures in which both orchestra and solo violin echo theme (a) conclude the first of the concerto's five sections .

Slowly

14 measures in 6/4 open this second section of 73 measures. Here we treat this as the development of a movement in sonata form. The violin expounds the strongly lyrical theme (f), characterised by the fusion of thematic elements from both themes (a) and (b). Four measures in 4/4 that present theme (g) follow.

theme (f)

theme (g)

Theme (f) is developed by the soloist over 16 measures in 4/4 time. They are followed by four measures in which the oboe and then the violin expound theme (g).

With the new exposition of theme (f) in 13 6/4 measures we arrive at another transition, marking the conclusion of this second section. It is a moment in which theme (g) is affirmed by both the soloist and the orchestra and it occurs over 22 4/4 measures.

Ad libitum

At this point in the concerto Delius inserts a new, dreamy cadenza accompagnata in 30 4/4 measures. Here the violinist, called on to interpret 14 variations on theme (a), is sustained harmonically by strings and flutes .

"Delius used to improvise *harmonically* on the violin, in *arpeggios outlining chords*, and this cadenza is no doubt a formalized example of the fantastic and wonderful harmonic arabesques he used to draw from the instrument."[66]

The 28th measure, shifting to 7/4 time so as to present three descending, chromatic sextuplets. is followed by a measure of four ascending quatrains in 4/4. The cadenza concludes with a measure in 6/4 in which the solo violin, supported by winds playing descending arpeggios, resolves in a unison recapitulation of theme (a).

Tempo I

The fourth section, composed of 61 measures, opens with a recapitulation of the first exposition's thematic group, unvaried in the first 14 measures. Following are 15 measures in 4/4 in which the solo violin develops theme (a), two measures in 12/8 in which the winds return to theme (d) and a measure, still in 12/8, in which the orchestra re-invokes theme (b).

The solo violin then moves us to the transition with a new version of theme (d1), six measures in 4/4, and proceeding with the exposition of theme (d) over two 12/8 measures. The section begins its conclusion with a new development of theme (a) that takes place over three measures in 4/4. Finally the second thematic group is recapitulated over 11 measures in 4/4 time. Brass and orchestra provide a re-exposition of theme (e) that also sees the soloist interjecting with quatrains, triplets and ascending split octaves.

Allegretto

The fifth and last section, 83 measures long, opens with the exposition of theme (h): eight measures in 12/8 in which string pizzicatos are accompanied by the soloist's sextuplets.

---

[66] ivi pp.260.

theme (h)

pizz.

Seven measures in 4/4 follow. Here the violin presents theme (j) and echoes theme (g). There are six measures in 12/8, the final in 6/8, in which the violin develops theme (j) and then nine more measures in 4/4, which represent the original elements of theme (j).

theme (j)

A measure in 12/8 serves as a connecter. The violin, supported by horns, here gives way to a 27 measure re-exposition of theme (h), in 12/8, by the orchestra. In the final four it is the violin who plays the theme.

The concerto finishes with a coda, 28 measures long, in 4/4 time. Here the violin re-proposes and combines the initial theme, (a), with theme (j) for an elegiac and delicate finale.

In concluding this analysis we can confirm Delius as having structured his Violin Concerto in a way that is extremely complex and articulated and that is "far from indulging in rhapsody."[67] Nevertheless we recognize that his work is based on clear, standard compositional principles (such as sonata form) and seeks out proportion as well as a complex equilibrium through the range of its five different sections.

The composer calls for the exposition of nine different themes in a continual flow of the melody and harmony, "while he is developing one he introduces another in the middle of that, and so on."[68]

Repeated changes in tempo (4/4 ,6/4, 12/8), frequent arpeggios and complex rhythmic patterns that feature triplets and sextuplets, chromaticism, bichords and split octaves render the soloist's score complex on a technical level. Delius had Albert Sammon's exceptional skill in mind when he conceived the part, "The function of the solo violin

---

[67] ivi pp.256.

[68] ivi pp.257.

is to sing and to decorate; chiefly to decorate. The difficulty of its part arises entirely from almost complete absence of familiar harmonies and intervals, and at no point is the difficulty connected with technical display."[69]

Great thought and attention to timbre and tessitura (and how these two interact) contribute to the creation of those multiple "atmospheres" that animate the concerto with not only intense and persuasive lyricism but also vibrant and stirring musical force.

Given its originality and unique character the Violin Concerto remains one of Delius' most seductive and fascinating works. For the composer "nothing is so wonderful as elemental feeling; nothing is more wonderful in art than elemental feeling expressed intensely."[70]

Comparative Study

We will now return to some of the specific stylistic components spoken about in connection with the four concertos studied thus far and in doing so draw a comparison and conclude this book's first section.

It is appropriate to reiterate the chronology of the concertos: Stanford's concerto (1899), Elgar's (1910), Coleridge-Taylor's (1912), and lastly that of Delius (1916). In a relatively brief period (17 years, and in the case of Elgar and Coleridge-Taylor almost overlapping) the four English composers had in common their decision to work on the same musical form, the violin concerto.

We should also keep in mind the "geography" of the concertos: Stanford in England, Elgar began in Italy and finished in England, Coleridge-Taylor in America and England and Delius in France.

The only concerto that was composed entirely in England was Stanford's. In all the other cases at least a part was written abroad (and in the case of Delius all of the concerto).

And finally we should keep in mind to whom the concertos were dedicated and by whom they were commissioned: Stanford dedicated his concerto to the Spanish violinist E.F. Arbòs; Elgar's concerto was both commissioned by and dedicated to Fritz Kreisler; Coleridge-Taylor's concerto was commissioned by Carl Stoecker and dedicated to the American violinist Maud Powell; the English violinist Albert Sammons, in the case of Delius, received the dedication.

---

[69] Donald Francis Tovey, *Essays in Music Analysis Vol. III Concertos,* pp.204.

[70] *Delius: A Life in Letters 1909-1934,* by Lionel Carley.

To these lists we should add some considerations that are of a more analytical character, comparing the key and the formal structure, of the individual concertos.

Stanford: D major/three movements: *Allegro, Canzona – Andante, Allegro Moderato.*

Elgar: B minor/three movements: *Allegro, Andante, Allegro molto.*

Coleridge-Taylor: G minor/three movements: *Allegro Maestoso – Vivace – Allegro Molto, Andante semplice – Andantino, Allegro molto - Moderato*

Delius: the key is never explicitly declared; five uninterrupted sections: *With moderate tempo, Slowly, Ad libitum, Tempo I, Allegretto.*

First of all we note how all the composers, with the exception of Delius, used a specific key and adopted the same formal structure, that of a concerto in three movements, typical of the 17th and 18th century compositional tradition.

Nevertheless, if we compare the individual movements of each concerto (leaving out, for the moment, Delius), we see how they were all conceived and therefore realized in different ways.

We will proceed in order, treating principally the first movement, returning to the schema and major characteristics of each concerto.

Regarding the internal structure of the movement, Stanford uses the traditional scheme of exposition, development, recapitulation, Elgar adopted the sonata form while Coleridge-Taylor, for his work, proposed three uninterrupted episodes.

Both Elgar and Coleridge-Taylor chose to begin the first movement with a more or less protracted tutti (69 and 31 measures, respectively) while Stanford presents a brief, four measure introduction constituted of pizzicato strings and winds.

Only Coleridge-Taylor provides a cadenza accompanied by timpani rolling on the dominant.

We will now consider the second movement.

Stanford utilizes the tripartite *canzone* structure while Elgar and Coleridge-Taylor employ the exposition-development-recapitulation scheme. The three incipits are similar: a brief orchestral exposition (in

Stanford played by clarinets and trombones) introducing the soloist's entrance. Only Stanford presents a long violin cadenza.

In each case the last movement is structured exposition-development-recapitulation and each begins with a brief orchestral introduction (eight measure in Stanford and Coleridge-Taylor and, for Elgar, just one). Only in the case of Elgar is there a cadenza present (accompanied by strings *tremolanti*, horns and timpani).

In closing this brief comparison we are able to affirm a substantial similarity in the macroscopic structure of the concertos (in three sections) and in the microscopic structure relating to the individual movements, each conceived and organized on the compositional scheme of exposition-development-recapitulation.

Nevertheless it is evident that each single composer "personalized" each movement with his own stylistic choices and different techniques, providing incipits of varying lengths, different quantities of thematic elements for each movement, the decision to include cadenzas (*accompagnata* or not), the maintenance (as in the case of Coleridge-Taylor) of a rhythmic linearity within each movement or the decision to not maintain such linearity.

In returning to Delius's violin concerto we will bring out the formal characterises and essential structures of the work's five uninterrupted sections.

This is the internal structure of the different sections:

With moderate tempo: much like the exposition of a first movement in sonata form, with a first thematic group, a transition passage and a second thematic group.

Slowly: similar to the development of a first movement in sonata form. *Ad libitum*: 14 variations on a theme.

Tempo I: much like the recapitulation of a first movement in sonata form

Allegretto: the exposition of a new thematic idea and coda.

Delius provides a cadenza accompagnata during the *Ad libitum* section.

The deep structural and stylistic differences of his concerto are evident from the outset. The composer, in seeking out that continuous flow of melody and harmony, which brought him to opt out of the traditional tripartite form, proposed a different type of score. It was an approach that sees the fullest expressions of its originality in the score's constant rhythmic alteration and continual harmonic transformation – qualities that required the composer to omit the work's key.

Certainly there is much more to say about these four concertos and the compositional techniques their composers adopted in creating them. We hope that what has been presented so far is nevertheless adequate for our purposes, that is to understand the context in which the violin concerto developed, in England, at the beginning of the 1900's. In so doing we have better understood some of the historical background that later gave life to William Walton's Violin Concerto, the work that is this book's focus.

We now proceed to those violin concertos written by British composers between 1920 and 1940.

PART II

Introduction

The 1920's and 30's in England were a period of intense social and cultural change. The transformations that the nation underwent were reflected, inevitably, also in its music.

The foundation of new musical and cultural institutions was one of the principle causes of the significant spread and promotion of classical music in the country.

The British Broadcasting Company (BBC), now Corporation, came into being in 1922 "bringing everyone the best performances of music from every school and period"[1]. The BBC also committed itself to the formation of its own professional orchestra.

In 1925, with the birth of the British Council, British artistic culture began reaching into territories outside the nation's borders, even if "other nations showed anxiety that we (the English) accepted various manifestations of their art according to their judgement, a proud "take it or leave it"[2] was the general British attitude" In the same year Covent Garden's Royal Opera House resumed its activities (interrupted during the years of WWI), cantering its interests on German, rather than Italian, opera.

On January 6th, 1931, the old suburban theatre Sadler's Wells also reopened. The theatre alternated between performances of Shakespeare and opera (and eventually also ballet).

Professional orchestras formed in all the country's major cities: Birmingham, Manchester, Bournemouth and London where, in 1932, Sir Thomas Beecham founded the London Philharmonic Orchestra, allied with the London Symphony Orchestra "reorganized under pressure from the new competition"[3]

Among the most characteristic cultural activities of the 19th century, which carried over into the 20th, were the great regional festivals. Some notable names are the Gloucester, Worcester and Hereford Three Choir

---

[1] Edward Lockspeiser, *UTET*, pp.395.
[2] Eric Blom, *Music in England,* La Nuova Italia, 1966, pp.220.
[3] ivi pp.219.

Festival and the Cheltenham Festival that had as "[its] sole duty the presentation of new English music for orchestra and chamber music, especially premiers"[4] Two other examples are the Edinburgh Festival and the National Fanfare Festival (for which Elgar, Holst and Vaughan Williams wrote pieces).

In the field of musical education new institutions, such as the Royal School of Church Music (founded in 1927 by Sir Sydney Nicholson) served alongside the more famous (i.e the Royal College of Music, the Royal Academy of Music and the universities of Oxford and Cambridge).

Journalism and music criticism received greater attention, in the 20's, with the birth of A.H. Fox Strangways' trimestral "Music & Letters," and with the articles and weekly music essays published in the newspapers: "The Times," "The Observer," "Sunday Times," "The Daily Telegraph," and "The Manchester Guardian" that was for years famous "for music criticism of the highest quality."[5]

The land without music, that many believed incapable of rehabilitation, demonstrated itself ready to begin a process of total regeneration that allowed it to definitively shake off that unfortunate label and become of the major players in 20th century music.

We have cited these developments as the principle factors in the shaping of English music sensibility. It was a sensibility that gave life to the music of the composers that we are about to discuss: Ralph Vaughan Williams, Arthur Somervell, Arnold Bax and Benjamin Britten, who we should mention was principally active between 1940 and 1975.

Within our analysis of their violin concertos we will treat their varying compositional poetics and so move towards a conclusion in which we will present a brief comparison of the different scores and approaches that influenced them.

Ralph Vaughan Williams

Ralph Vaughan Williams, Charles Robert Darwin's great-grandson, was born October 12th, 1872, in Down Ampney in Gloucestershire. He began as a piano student (under one of his aunts) and in 1887 attended (for three years) London's Charterhouse School. Her he took up the study of the violin and viola. Between 1890 and 1892 he attended the Royal College of Music and between 1893 and 1895 he worked for a Bachelor's

---

[4] ivi pp.218.
[5] ivi pp.231.

degree in music and history at Cambridge's Trinity College. In 1896 he returned to the Royal College in London to study composition with Charles Villiers Stanford, Hubert Parry and Charles Wood. In 1897 He also studied under Max Brunch, in Berlin and in 1908 in Paris with Maurice Ravel, who "could not have given more than a final touch to something that was already slowly materializing in him."[6]

After 1904, thanks to the economic security that relieved him of having to compose for necessity, Vaughan Williams dedicated himself to the study of traditional English music, accompanied in his ethno musicological research by his friend and colleague Gustav Holst, who he'd met in 1895 at the Royal College of Music.

The influence of this traditional music is particularly evident in certain pieces, such as the *Three Norfolk Rhapsodies* (1905-06), the *Five English Folk-songs* (1913) and the *Fantasia on "Greensleeves"* (1934, "but the most striking manifestation of Vaughan William's ability to absorb English folk music and make it part of his own musical idiom was not so much his use of actual folk melodies, but his capacity to make musical statements that sound as if they are of folk origin."[7]

At the age of 38 he made his public debut at the Leeds Festival (1910) with the choral symphony's performance of his *"The Sea Symphony."* The piece, based on Walt Whitman's poetry was the first and the longest of the composer's nine symphonies. In 1914, at London's Queen Hall, he presented the second symphony, *"A London Symphony"* directed by Geoffrey Toye.

With the outbreak of World War I Vaughan Williams decided to enlist as a volunteer in the Field Ambulance Service, in Belgium's Flanders region. In 1918 he returned to England and began teaching composition at the Royal College of Music. In 1920 he began directing with the Bach Choir.

In 1922 he finished his third symphony, titled *"A Pastoral Symphony"* and in 1925 he began work on the score of a suite for solo viola, *Flos Campi*, as well as the *Concerto for Violin and Strings*, which we will shortly treat. The 30's and 40's were for Vaughan Williams a period of maximum production and compositional experimentation, during which time he wrote the Symphonies four, five and six (called the *"Antarctic Symphony"*), the *Piano Concerto*, the *Oboe Concerto* and numerous choral pieces and music for film.

---

[6] Otto Karolyi, *Modern British Music,* pp.25.
[7] ivi pp.26.

In the '50s he began work on the eighth and ninth symphonies, on a cycle of songs for voice and oboe called *Ten Blake songs*, on two *Preludes* for organ and on the *Tuba Concerto*.

Ralph Vaughan Williams died on August 29th, 1958 at the age of 86. His ashes are held at Westminster, near the tombs of Henry Purcell and Charles Villiers Stanford.

Vaughan Williams' compositional poetic, as underlined by Otto Karolyi, appears to be the result of a complex fusion of diverse influences: "...from German and contemporary English music, as well as from the last of the great English composers before Elgar, Henry Purcell; from his deep understanding of the Tudor composers; from folk music, which he started collecting in 1902; and from his work as the editor of the English Hymnal (1906)."[8]

They are influences, however, that apart from Bach, Handel and Ravel, extend almost entirely from the British tradition. In a kind of conservative nationalism, Vaughan Williams saw himself as a guardian and rediscovered of that tradition: "so evident in those modalities deriving from the folk tradition and the 19th century techniques of the Pastoral Symphony (1922) and Symphony No. Four (1935)."[9]

Despite the fact that the ideas expressed in this book are in agreement with Edward Neill, we should take note of how the influx of traditional music, channelled through Vaughan Williams' work, modified (maybe unconsciously) the structure of the English symphony, moving it away from the norms of the classical form in favour a form that is more freely rhapsodic.

The "grand old man"[10] of English music, who affirmed that "if the foundation of our art is rooted in the same soil and only this soil possesses something original to give you, you can always gain the entire world with losing your souls"[11] though he wed himself to a past musical tradition was nevertheless capable of creating a personal and original musical language, thanks in part to his employment of unusual instrumental formations (such as the brief Romance composition, for harmonica and string orchestra). This personal language has long been held (as surely would have pleased the composer) as representative of what the first half of the 20th century had to offer in terms of authentic English musical feeling. "The composer

---

[8] ivi pp.25.

[9] Jonathan Cross, *da Compositori e Istituzioni in Inghilterra,* pp.473   Enciclopedia della Musica, Einaudi.

[10] ivi pp.474.

[11] Vaughan Williams, *National Music 1934,* in *National Music and Other Essays,* Oxford University Press, London.

doesn't have to isolate himself and think only of art, but must live with his peers and render his art and expression of the whole community's life"[12]

Concerto for Violin and Strings in D Minor
"Concerto Accademico"

Ralph Vaughan Williams wrote his violin concerto between 1924 and 1925 and dedicated it to the Hungarian violinist Jelly d'Aranyi, the same violinist to whom Ravel dedicated Tzigane. The origin of the title "Concerto Accademica" refers to the composer's desire to use the 18th century model of composition, particularly that of J.S. Bach. The decision to employ an orchestra composed only of strings is a clear testimony to this stylistic choice.

The Concerto Accademico "is an engaging work, a tightly-wrought synthesis of neo-classicism, folk-dance rhythms and triadic harmony."[13]

First movement. *Allegro pesante*

The concerto opens with an affirmation of theme (a) by the soloist and orchestra. The theme's rhythmic pattern clearly recalls the first movement of Bach's Violin Concerto in A minor BWV 1041.

theme (a)

theme (a1)

A brief episode, almost a cadenza, follows, in which the violin plays semichromatic quatrains on intervals of fourths and fifths (theme (b)) sustained by an accompaniment of chords and pizzicatos.

---

[12] Ralph Vaughan Williams, *da R.V. Williams,* Hubert Foss 1950, pp.200 1950.
[13] Michael Kennedy, *The Works of Ralph Vaughan Williams,* 1980.

theme (b)

The orchestra begins with a brief fragment of theme (a), then moves to a clear re-exposition of theme (a1). An episode in 3/4 concludes the exposition "with a dialogue in which the soloist's double stopped sixths are answered by theme (a1)." [14]

The development, first in 2/4 time, opens with the strings' re-exposition, in counterpoint, of themes (a) and (b). This is followed by the solo violin's re-elaboration of theme (a).

An orchestral tutti re-proposes theme (a1) to which the violin then responds first with chords of thirds and then with a cadenza accompagnata, bringing about a new 3/4 episode. "The double stopped sixths bridge the way to the recapitulation".[15] The episode's coda concludes with a resolution, a trill by the soloist and orchestra.

Second movement. *Adagio*

A solo by cello, theme (a), accompanied by muted strings, introduces the violin's entrance. The entrance signals a rapid shift from a minor mode to a major.

theme (a)

A varied accompaniment of second violins and violas that is "thoroughly Bach-like in spirit"[16] then sustains the soloist's new melodic pattern, theme (b), which is constituted of a series of ascending scales imitated by first violins and solo cello.

---

[14] William Mann, *Some English Concertos,* pp.423, The Concerto by Ralph Hill.
[15] ivi pp.423.
[16] ivi 424.

theme (b)

A re-exposition follows in which the violin presents theme (a) and then theme (b). The episode moves towards a dreamy finale, which concludes in the key of G major.

Third movement, *Presto*

The final movement "demonstrates that Bach was not Vaughan Williams' only model for solo violin writing…now the fiddle element bursts out in a jig tune hewn from a convivial moment in the opera *Hugh the Drover*."[17]

theme (a)

The violin opens the *Presto* finale with descending and ascending thirds (a) and then moves towards a jig. During this more ordered passage the violin is first accompanied by pizzicatos and then by the violas' recapitulation. A new exposition of (a)'s thematic elements and of the jig follows – the phrases are now more developed and re-elaborated.

theme (c)

---

[17] Stephen Banfield, Booklet EMI cd, 2000.

Theme (c), a *cantabile*, comes next. It is briefly presented by the solo only to be immediately interrupted by the orchestra's re-exposition of theme (b). The concerto closes with a final "ruminatory cadenza"[18] by the solo violin, on the initial theme (a), in the concerto's original key, D minor.

And so we come to understand that the "Concerto Accademico" came to represent an example of absolute originality among English violin concertos at the beginning of the 20th century. For this work Ralph Vaughan Williams adopted a hybrid compositional style that combined his personal poetic, often characterized by traditional/folk elements, with a Bachian criteria whose origins lie in the 1700's.

The result of this unique synthesis was a concerto for a solo instrument and string orchestra (unusual for a period in which a symphonic orchestra was the orchestra of choice) , written in the tripartite form with the first movement in sonata form and the final a jig, that concludes with a surprising dispersion.

The "Concerto Accademico" was not conceived as a mere amusement or artificial experiment. On the contrary it is the product of an individual, personal style that maintains an awareness of what it is doing. It is a style to which the critic William Mann tied the verdian motto "Let us go back to the past, it will be a step forward."

Arthur Somervell

Born in Windermere on June 5th, 1863, in the English country of Cumbria, Arthur Somervel was first educated at the Uppingham School and then at the King's College of Cambridge University where he was a student of Charles Villiers Stanford. From 1883 to 1885 he attended the Hochschule fur Musik in Berlin, going on to study composition between 1885 and 1887 with Hubert Parry at London's Royal College of Music (where he himself began teaching in 1894).

He served as the Inspector of Music to the Board of Education between 1901 and 1928 and, after 1929 (the year in which he was knighted by King George V) as president of the Royal School of Church Music.

Arthur Somervell is often remembered as a composer of songs. He is celebrated for his five song cycles *Maud* (1898), *Love in Springtime* (1901), *A Shropshire Lad* (1904), *James Lee's Wife* (1908), *A Broken Arc*

---

[18] William Mann, *Some English Concertos*, pp.425.

(1923) and his choral works, such as *A Song of Praise* (1891) and *The Passion of Christ* (1914).

Among his major orchestral works are the orchestral ballad *Helen of Kirkconnell* (1893), the *Thalassa Symphony* (1912), the concerto for piano *"The Highland"* (1921) and the *Violin Concerto* (1932), which we will discuss shortly.

Despite his being a dominant figure in that period of English music, Somervell is not considered an original composer. In fact his music was defined as being "grounded in the German classics, lying somewhere between Mendelssohn and Brahms in an area which was perhaps more adequately explored by Parry."[19]

Concerto for Violin and Orchestra in G Minor

Somervell wrote the Violin Concerto in 1930 and dedicated it to the violinist Adila Fachiri, Joseph Joachim's great-granddaughter and the sister of Jelly d'Arany (to whom Vaughan Williams dedicated his Concerto Accademico). The first public performance took place in 1932, in Edinburgh, with the Reid Orchestra directed by Mary Grierson. The BBC Symphony Orchestra, led by Adrian Boult, performed the concerto in February of 1933 and "it was quickly heard in various provincial concerts including Liverpool and twice in Bournemouth"[20]

Despite the publication of both the concerto's score as well as an abridged version for piano, the work remained largely forgotten. Attention was once again paid to the concerto when in 2005 the violinist Martyn Brabbins recorded it.

First movement, *Allegro moderato e con grazia*

The concerto opens with a protracted tutti in which first theme (a), in 6/8 time, is presented, then theme (b) in 2/4 and finally theme (c) in 3/4. At this point the violinist enters with a passage that closely resembles a cadenza.

---

[19] Michael Hurd, *The New Groove of Music and Musicians*, pp.665.
[20] Lewis Foreman, Hyperion Booklet cd, 2005.

theme (a)

theme (b)

theme (c)

The soloist then proceeds with the re-exposition of theme (a) accompanied by pizzicatos and winds and a presentation of theme (d) "this leads through one or two new incidents to a regular solo version of the whole second group"[21] themes (b) and (c).

A variation of theme (a), that we will call (a1), precedes a new tutti that signals the beginning of the development in the key of B flat minor. Here all the thematic material is re-elaborated.

The recapitulation is introduced by a new exposition of theme (a), now in a major key, then theme (d) in the key of E minor. Theme (a1) follows and at its conclusion the soloist's cadenza begins. For some central measures its is accompanied by muted strings who echo theme (b).

theme (d)

theme (a1)

[21] Donald Francis Tovey, *Essays in Music Analysis Vol. III Concertos,* pp.161.

A serene and melodic coda once again recalls theme (a), in a major key, only to then move, energetically, towards the finale in which "the theme returns to its original heroic mood."[22]

Second Movement, *Adagio*

Four measures of solo winds introduce the violin's entrance, which presents the movement's principle theme (a). A passage that modulates between E flat and G major follows.

theme (a)

First winds and then the soloist play theme (b), which will be followed by the recapitulation, the re-exposition of theme (a) and a coda that concludes in the key of E flat major.

theme (b)

Third movement, *Allegro giocoso*

The last movement, in G major, a rondo, opens with the violin's exposition of theme (a). An episode in which the soloist and then the orchestra present theme (b), moving from the key of F major to the original key of G major. Here the orchestra seems "to stretch itself in a slow yawn while the solo violin blows smoke-rings"[23]

theme (a)

---

[22] ivi pp.162.
[23] ivi pp.163.

theme (b)

After a complex development section it is the trumpet who announces the return of theme (a), and so opens the recapitulation. A coda, echoing the first movement of Mendelssohn's Violin Concerto (a pattern of ascending triplets), energetically concludes the work, once again in the key of G major.

"While Somervell was a product of a Germanic musical aesthetic, there is an English feel to this music which Tovey ascribed to the treatment of the minor mode which is tinged with the Doric and Aeolian of English and kindred folk- song."[24]

Donald Francis Tovey, with whom Mary Grierson studied at the University of Edinburg, recognized the English character of Somervell's Violin Concerto. Somervells work echoes the pastoral episodes of Vaughan Williams and the lyricism of Elgar, "while the key-system of the whole work is by no means tied down to classical precedent." [25]

Despite the brevity and incompleteness of our analysis, we believe it to be nevertheless comprehensible (thanks in part to Tovey's reflections), how Somervell's concerto is not exclusively tied to the scores and styles of German composers such as Brahms and Mendelssohn.

On the contrary, given the concerto's employment of such original compositional techniques, Arthur Somervell's work appears to be the result of the desire to achieve a personal language that is capable of expressing "English feeling."

---

[24] Lewis Foreman, Hyperion Booklet cd, 2005.
[25] Donald Francis Tovey, *Essays in Music Analysis Vol. III Concertos,* pp.159.

Arnold Bax

Sir Arnold Edward Trevor Bax was born in London on November 8th, 1883. He first attended the Heath Mount School and the Hampstead Conservatory, where he studied under Cecil James Sharp. In 1900 he enrolled at the Royal Academy of Music. Here he studied, until 1905, composition with Frederick Corder and piano with Tobia Matthay.

Young Bax maintained a love of literature and writing that ran parallel to his passion for music. He was particularly inspired by the Irish poet William Butler Yeats and the Norwegian poet Bjørnstjerne Bjørnson. It was "after reading Yeats's The Wanderings of Oisin, that Bax virtually trained himself to "become" Irish, and based one of his tone poems, (a genre that particularly suited him), In the Faery Hills (1909), on Yeats's work."[26]

Other works, whose celtic and nordic atmospheres indicate literary influences on Bax's music are *The Flute* (1907), An *Irish Elegy* (1907) and *Hardanger* (1927).

Works such as the two *Russian Tone-Pictures* (1911) and *In a Vodka Shop* (1915) recall Russian and Slavic music, with which the composer had had contact during his travels in the Ukraine in 1910.

Together with his wife Elsita Sobrino (who Bax married in 1911), the composer moved to Dublin where, under the pseudonym Dermot O'Byrne, he entered George William Russell's literary circle.

During the years of the first World War Bax returned to London, and dedicated himself to writing his First Symphony, completed in 1922, and to composing some symphonic poems, such as *Summer Music* (1916), *Tintagel* and *November Woods* (both 1917).

After the war, and until the outbreak of the second World War, the composer travelled every year to a small village in Scotland, Morar, where he found inspiration for the composition of many of his symphonies (seven in all) and in particular for the *Northern Ballads*.

In 1937 he received the "Knight Bachelor," in 1942 he was nominated Master of the King's Music and in 1953 Knight Commander of the Royal Victorian Order.

Arnold Bax died in Cork on October 3rd, 1953.

---

[26] Otto Karolyi, *Modern British Music,* pp.21.

Concerto for Violin and Orchestra

Between 1937 and March of 1938 Bax worked on the composition of his Violin Concerto, written "for Heifetz (as the dedication "For Firenze" on the manuscript testifies) but according to William Walton, Heifetz found the music disappointing. Presumably it was not sufficiently virtuosic."[27]

Walton's 1939 Violin Concerto, as we will read in this book's third section, was written for and dedicated to Jascha Heifetz.

Bax had to wait until 1942 to see his concerto made public. In that year it was performed by the violinist Eda Kersey and the BBC Symphony Orchestra directed by Sir Henry Wood.

"Certainly the work marks a new approach for Bax: comparatively lightly scored, it is charming and romantic in contrast to the Sturm und Drang of the symphonies. When asked to describe it, he remarked "Well I suppose it's rather like Raff", possibly referring to the Raff of the Cavatina rather than the symphonies" [28] (Joseph Joachim was a 19th century Swiss composer and pianist)

First movement, *Ouverture, ballad and Scherzo. Allegro Risoluto – Allegro moderato – Poco Largamente*

The concerto's first movement is structured in three uninterrupted sections. The orchestra opens with an exposition of theme (a), that in certain measures seems to echo the first movement of Walton's First Symphony (written in 1935). The violin then enters, elaborating the thematic material until arriving at a brief exposition of a melody in thirds. This is then interrupted for the climactic return of theme (ac), then concluded with a new, energetic tutti, the first of three episodes.

theme (a)

[27] Lewis Foreman, Chandos Booklet CD, 1991.
[28] ibidem.

In the second episode, *ballad* "evocative harp chords set the scene , but the melody is accompanied delicately by woodwind with un easy string asides"[29].

The solo then plays the melodic theme (b), followed by the rhythmically varied (b1). The latter takes place in the second of the ballad's four stanzas. The final stanza precedes the *Scherzo*.

theme (b)

theme (b1)

Four harp chords introduce the solo with "a jovial jig version"[30] of theme (a). It is accompanied alternately by strings and by winds. The orchestra offers variations on themes (a) and (b), to which the violin responds with a virtuosistic, "dancing" melodic line. A final passage recalling jazz music brings the movement to a luminous close in the key of E major.

Second movement, *Adagio*

Solo strings, with accompaniment by the harp, open the concerto's second movement. This exposition of theme (a) "alludes to the Elgar Violin Concerto, thus the shape of the music might also be construed as a reference to his friend Benjamin Dale's Piano Sonata of 1905." [31]

[29] William Mann, *Some English Concertos*, pp.406.
[30] ivi pp.407.
[31] Lewis Foreman, Chandos Booklet CD, 1991.

theme (a)

A solo by clarinets introduce the violin who plays theme (a) on its G string, accompanied by solo winds. Theme (b), cantabile, is then announced, first by the soloist and then by a tutti *fortissimo*.

theme (b)

The orchestra returns to the initial theme (a), also elaborated by the soloist. Upon finishing the soloist revisits, now in a lower register, theme (b), until vanishing "on a soft bed of muted horn tune."[32]

Third movement, *Allegro*

The last movement opens with theme (a), played by the violinist who is accompanied by pizzicato strings and a Basque tambourine. After a variation the theme's original form is affirmed by an orchestral tutti.

theme (a)

Passing through another elaboration on theme (a) the soloist first moves on to an exposition of theme (d), a waltz, and then into a development episode, concluded by theme (a)'s return, now in 9/8 time. Here the "figuration becomes more urgent and the soloist bursts into a

---

[32] William Mann, *Some English Concertos*, pp.408.

rushing virtuoso passage that is the nearest approach to a cadenza in this concerto."[33]

theme (b)

From an orchestral tutti of theme (b) the soloist shifts to a new exposition of theme (a), in the theme's original meter and so comes to conclude the concerto in the key of E major.

Bax's Concerto for Violin and Orchestra, another concerto that deserves more attention than what has been paid it, presents clear, distinctive elements. The tripartition of the first movement into Ouverture, ballad, and Scherzo, as well as the absence of an *authentic* cadenza represent clear examples of such a deliberate design.

Absolute stylistic variety, from Elgarian lyricism to the Straussian waltz, from the jazz atmosphere to brilliant virtuosism, render each of the concerto's three movements an original achievement. The concerto's composition coincides with William Walton's Violin Concerto and so we will return to the work in this book's third section.

Benjamin Britten

The last composer treated in this book's second part is Benjamin Edward Britten.

The son of a dentist and amateur musician, Britten was born November 22nd, 1913, in Lowestoft, Suffolk. He was educated at Holt's Gresham's School in Norfolk. His music studies began first with his mother and then with the composer Frank Bridge who "quickly realised what was there; he was soon generously describing Britten's gifts by a larger title than mere talent."[34]

He attended the Royal College of Music from 1930 to 1933. There Britten studied composition with John Ireland and piano with Arthur Benjamin. Despite his progress during that period the young Britten found

---

[33] ivi pp.409.
[34] Scott Goddard, *British Music of Our Time*, pp.209.

himself troubled by "the low status music had in Britain and how oppressive militant officials of parochialism could be."[35]

Britten was nevertheless able to find the inspiration for his first works, like the *Sinfonietta* Op. 1 for chamber orchestra and the *Phantasy Quartet* for oboe and strings (both written in 1932). *A Boy Was Born* Op. 3 for choir and the *Simple Symphony* for string orchestra came later, in 1934.

In 1935 he met and befriended the Anglo-American poet W.H. Auden with whom he collaborated for the realization of the song cycle "Our Hunting Fathers," presented at the Norwich Festival in 1936. The work "amused the sophisticated, scandalised those among the gentry who caught Auden's words, and left musicians dazzled at so much talent, uneasy that it should be expended on so arid a subject, not knowing whether to consider Britten's daring style as the outcome of courage or foolhardiness."[36]. In the same year he met the man who became his collaborator and life-partner, the tenor Peter Pears.

In 1939, shortly after the outbreak of World War I, Britten and Pears, along with Auden and their friend Christopher Isherwood, left for America where the composer wrote the *Diversions* Op. 21 for piano, dedicated to Paul Wittgenstein, the song cycle *Les Illuminations* Op. 18, *Seven Sonnets of Michelangelo* Op. 22, the choral works *Hymn to St. Cecilia* Op. 27 (using Auden's text) and *A Ceremony of Carols* Op. 28, and finally the *Violin Concerto* Op. 15, which we will discuss shortly. We should keep in mind that in America, in 1939, William Walton was putting the finishing touches on *his* violin concerto as well.

"The three years that Britten spent in America made him realize where his roots were. The uprooted state of an émigré did not suit him: he did not share Stravinsky's cosmopolitan savoir faire; he needed his national roots."[37] And so in 1942 Britten decided to return to England where he worked on arranging a series of traditional songs, later collected in the three volumes *British, French, British.*

On June 7th, 1945, Britten's *Peter Grimes* opened at London's Sadler's Wells. The opera, which uses Montagu Slater's libretto (based on "The Borough" by the English poet George Crabbe) pushed Britten into the limelight, making him the most "representative" of the post-World War II British composers.

---

[35] Otto Karolyi, *Modern British Music,* pp. 59.
[36] Scott Goddard, *British Music of Our Time,* pp.211.
[37] Otto Karolyi, *Modern British Music,* pp.62.

In 1946 Britten composed the *Young Person's Guide to the Orchestra* Op. 34 (using a theme by Purcell) and the opera *The Raper of Lucretia* Op. 37 (using Ronald Duncan's libretto). These were followed, in 1948, by *Albert Herring* Op. 39 (adapted from Maupassant's "Le Rosier de Mme"), in 1951 by *The Beggar's Opera*, *Billy Budd*, and in 1954 by *The Turn of the Screw*.

In 1957 Britten and Pears returned from a trip to Asia. Britten, inspired from his travels, wrote the ballet The *Prince of the Padagos* and the semi-operas *Parables for Church Perfomance.*

The November 14th bombardment of the Coventry Cathedral had forced its closure in 1940. Britten marked the occasion its re-opening on May 30th, 1962, with the first public performance of his celebrated *War Requiem*. His 1973 opera *Death in Venice* and his 1976 cantata for mezzo soprano and orchestra *Phaedra* remain among his most important later works.

Britten died on December 4th, 1976, at Alderburgh in Suffolk. In life the English composer had put his mind to work on a huge variety of musical genres and forms, from opera to ballet, from the solistic concerto to symphonic and chamber works, from vocal and choral music to music for film.

His use of different compositional techniques and methods ensured that his scores were constantly evolving, from one to the next. The result was not an affected or forced sort of experimentation but rather a sense of his continual desire to seek out "original" artistry

"Variations writing, which with the use of patterns reiterated as accompaniment and background are the two method often employed by Britten"[38] . But Britten's excursions into a range of artistic territories also brought him to the use of atonalism (such as *Turn of the Screw*) and expressionism (with the *Sinfonietta*).

It is difficult to do justice to as productive and eclectic composer as Britten, in so little space. However as Walton, and his Violin Concerto, are the focus of this book we are forced to limit this kind of biographic material to a basic outline, that is, to provide just enough of a background to contextualize the compositional poetic that operates in the concerto subsequently analyzed.

---

[38] Scott Goddard, *British Music of Our Time*, pp.210.

Concerto for Violin and Orchestra OP.15

The Violin Concerto "is Britten's first major work to get written on the other side of the Atlantic Ocean."[39] This fact is indicated in the manuscript, completed on June 18th, 1939 during a stay in St. Jovite in Quebec, Canada.

Dedicated to Henry Boyss, an old friend of the composer, the concerto saw its first public performance on March 28th, 1940 at New York's Carnegie Hall. The Spanish violinist Antonio Brosa served as soloist. He was accompanied by the New York Philharmonic Orchestra, directed by John Barbirolli.

"The performance exceeded all expectations. Brosa's wife reported the gratifying amount of applause, and Britten himself wrote Hawkes, "John B. was very serious and took great pains over it – and the orchestra liked playing it a lot."[40]

The first performance in the United Kingdom took place on April 6th, 1941, at London's Queen's Hall with Thomas Matthews as violinist and the BBC Northern Orchestra, directed by Charles Groves, accompanying.

In October of 1950 Britten made some small structural changes to the score. In 1954 he and the Turkish violinist Manoug Parikian revisited also the violin part, taking out Brosa's corrections and simplifying some figurations.

Before beginning an analysis of the concerto we would like to make note of the orchestra's scoring: three flutes, two piccolos, two oboes, an English horn, two clarinets, two bassoons, four horns, three trumpets, three trombones, a tuba, timpani, glockenspiel, triangle, snares, bass drum, tenor drum, cymbals, harp and strings.

"Brosa believed that the rhythmic figure on the timpani which opens the concerto and often recurs was Spanish in origin and that the whole work represented Britten's response to the Spanish Civil war. Britten, influenced by his teacher and mentor Frank Bridge, was a lifelong pacifist."[41]

---

[39] David Ewen, *The World of Twentieth Century Music*.

[40] Suzanne Robinson, *"An English Composer Sees America": Benjamin Britten and the North American Press,1939-1942*, *American Music,Vol.15*, No.3 (1997) pp.327.

[41] Michael Kennedy, EMI Booklet CD, 1992.

First movement, *Moderato con moto*

The Concerto opens with a brief introduction in which the timpani foreshadow the bassoon's and horn's rhythmic pattern in what will be their accompaniment to the chromatic theme (a). The ninth measure sees the violin's exposition of the theme: "Brosa believed that the rhythmic figure on the timpani which opens the concerto and often recurs was Spanish in origin and that the whole work represented Britten's response to the Spanish Civil war. Britten, influenced by his teacher and mentor Frank Bridge, was a lifelong pacifist."[42]

theme (a)

A brief cadenza by the soloist concludes with a new exposition, now by the orchestra, of theme (a). The soloist then presents theme (b), *agitato* but expressive, "over a chorale-like accompaniment in muted horns"[43]

theme (b)

The elaboration of this thematic material itself concludes with a clear declaration of theme (a), by the orchestra. The episodes signals the beginning of a recapitulation, in which the solo violin repeats the timpani' initial rhythmic pattern. The movement then closes with an extensive coda, by the soloist, accompanied by timpani.

---

[42] Michael Kennedy, EMI Booklet CD, 1992
[43] David Ewen, *The World of Twentieth Century Music.*

Second movement. *Vivace*

The concerto's second movement is a scherzo. "If Walton's scherzo is a tarantella. Britten's is a dance with death of a grimmer kind, the soloist executing brilliant and grotesque feats of virtuosity."[44]

theme (a)

The violin's rhythmic chords and *agitato* orchestral figurations introduce theme (a), presented by the soloist over bassoons.

A presentation of theme (b) follows with the trio section in A minor. This concludes with a tuba solo, piccolos and the soloist's new exposition of theme (a).

theme (b)

Theme (b), performed by an energetic tutti orchestra, comes to a close with the cadenza's onset. Here the violin re-elaborates the themes and rhythmic patterns both of the first and second movements. It also foreshadows those of the third, which follows without interruption.

Third movement, *Passacaglia (Andante lento – Un poco meno mosso)*

The trombones, who have remained silent up until this point, emerge with the cadenza's close. They play the passacaglia theme (a), constituted of a scale that alternates in ascending and descending patterns.

---

[44] Michael Kennedy, EMI Booklet CD, 1992.

theme (a)

Nine variations follow:

- *con moto*, figurations by the violin soloist accompanied by tremolo strings
- *pesante*, here the winds offer the theme, adorned by the soloist, on a C pedal tone
- *tranquillo*, the oboe is the soloist, with orchestra accompanying
- *con moto*, the violinist again takes up the melody, now rhythmically free, over an accompaniment in 3/4 time.
- The violin and winds alternate between theme and accompaniment, on an F pedal tone
- A march on a C pedal tone
- *molto animato*, bassoons carry the theme, adorned by the violinist on an E pedal tone
- *largamente,* a tutti
- *lento e solenne*, the soloist is accompanied by the orchestra with a sequence of dark chords

After the violin provides the climax, a passage played on the G string, it goes on to conclude the concerto with a trill on an unfretted D chord, without any median interval by the orchestra.

Britten first met the Spanish violinist Antonio Brosa for the occasion of the concert in April of 1936. The event took place as part of the International Society for Contemporary Music Festival, in Barcelona. The composer accompanied Brosa on the piano, for the first public performance of his *Suite* Op. 6.

The festival's program also provided for the world premier of a Violin Concerto by Alban Berg, the composer who had passed away on December of 1935.

"It is tempting to infer that Britten might have been inspired to compose his own concerto after hearing the Berg performance, but apart from sharing a predominately sombre, elegiac atmosphere , the two works have little in common."[45]

---

[45] Lloyd Moore, NAXOS Booklet CD, 2005.

Certainly another source of inspiration for the composer was the Spanish political situation in those years, marked by the rise of a fascist dictator and the imminent outbreak of a civil war.

"In this respect, the *Violin Concerto* follows in the line of other Britten works from this period, including *Our Hunting fathers*, the *Ballad of Heroes* and the *Sinfonia da Requiem*, in which he gave artistic expression to his growing awareness and anxiety at developing world events."[46]

An awareness of these facts certainly helps us to better understand the distinctive features of a concerto conceived in Spain and *for* Spain and then finalized in America.

It is in this way that we come to understand the significance of the timpani's initial rhythmic pattern, of the frenetic dance and the second movement's gypsy melodies, of the finale's weeping emotional intensity as transmitted through the violin's fourth string.

The concerto, for its richness in specific extra musical meaning, presents a number of original compositional methods.

The first movement "is a prime example of Britten's highly original rethinking of sonata-form"[47] in the recapitulation the composer does not present anew the second subject. In place of the traditional second movement *lento*, Britten preferred a scherzo (the initial theme of which strongly recalls the second movement of Sergei Prokofiev's Concerto for Violin and Orchestra No. 1, also a scherzo). This movement is tied to the successive movement by an extended cadenza and so one movement passes to another without interruption. Finally the decision to found the third movement on the passacaglia form represents an unconventional variation method.

Britten was 26 when he finished composing the concerto, which belongs to his early period but already displays his notable technical-compositional skill and a full maturity of artistic thought. "It is cruel, you know, that music should be so beautiful. It has the beauty of loneliness and of pain: of strength and freedom. The beauty of disappointment and never-satisfied love. The cruel beauty of nature, and everlasting beauty of monotony."[48]

---

[46] Ibidem.
[47] Ibidem.
[48] Benjamin Britten, Letter of 29th June 1937; in "Letters from a Life: Letters and Diaries of Benjamin Britten" vol. 1, "A Working Life," 1991.

Comparative Study

In concluding this book's second part we will now present a brief comparative study that will permit us to evaluate, through a comparative lense, the four concertos analyzed.

We begin by reiterating the chronological order, the "when:" Vaughan Williams (1925), Somervell (1930), Bax (1938), Britten (1939).

We have four different violin concertos written in the arch of 14 years, two of these (Bax and Britten) were finalized within a year of each other.

The "where" of the works is as follows: England for Williams, Somervell and Bax. Britten began work on his concerto in Spain and finished it in America.

It's appropriate to make note of how the better part of these works were written on British soil, in contrast to the first four concertos analyzed.

Finally the "who," that is to whom the concertos were dedicated (none of the four was really commissioned): Vaughan Williams dedicated his concerto to the Hungarian violinist Jelly d'Aranyl, Somervell dedicated his to Adia Fachiri, a student of Joseph Joachim; Bax dedicated his to Jascha Heifetz and Britten to Henry Boys.

All the concertos except in the case of Britten were dedicated to violinists. Bax's concerto was never played by Jascha Heifetz.

Now we will consider some characteristics that are of a more strictly analytical nature, highlighting the keys and formal structures of the individual concertos.

Vaughan Williams: D minor/three movements: *Allegro pesante, Adagio, Presto*

Somervell: G minor/three movements: *Allegro moderato e con grazia, Adagio, Allegro giocoso*

Bax: the key is not explicitly declared/three movements: *Ouverture-ballad – Scherzo, Adagio, Allegro*

Britten: the key is not explicitly declared/Moderato con moto, Vivace, Passacaglia

It's important to note how only two of the four composers, Vaughan Williams and Somervell, declare their concerto's key but that all four adopt the same, tripartite formal structure.

We will now move to a more detailed comparison of the concertos' individual movements and so establish the ways in which they correspond.

Within the internal structure of each concerto's first movement a tripartite structure was also adopted. This structure is founded on the exposition-development-recapitulation scheme, though Bax uses the terms "ouverture," "ballad" and "scherzo" to organize the movement.

The incipit of each movement is characterized by a more or less protracted tutti that also introduces the violin soloist. This is true in each case except for Williams' concerto where the soloist and orchestra expound the principle theme together, a decision that was in accordance with 18th century musical tradition.

In each movement we also note a certain rhythmic variety coinciding with a thematic or episodic change. Only Britten chose to maintain the same meter throughout the entire movement. The thematic material usually consists of two or four elements.

Finally we should make note of the fact that Somervell was the only composer who decided to include a cadenza in his concerto's first movement.

Moving on to the second movement: all are structured as slow *adagio* movements in the tripartite exposition-development-recapitulation form except for Britten's *Vivace*. A cello solo and flute solo open the concertos of Williams and Somervell, respectively, a tutti opens Bax's and a brief passage played by first violins and cellos open Britten's.

There is no rhythmic variety, except some metric changes in the case of Britten, who is also the only composer who included a cadenza. Each concerto presents two thematic elements.

Finally we will move on to the third movements.

Once again we should distinguish the internal formal structure of Britten's third movement, with its particular nine variations on a passacaglia. Otherwise the concertos are founded on the usual exposition-development-recapitulation scheme.

The soloist opens the final movement in the case of Vaughan Williams, Somervell and Britten while Bax chose to employ a tutti for the occasion. Rhythmic variety *is* present in Bax's and Britten's third movements while the meter remains unmodified in the cases of Vaughan Williams and Somervell.

Two thematic elements are offered by Somervell and Bax, three by Vaghan Williams and one, with variations, by Britten.

There is a cadenza in the third movement of only Vaughan Williams' Concerto Accademico.

Despite their having shared certain decisions, we come to understand how the four composers structured their concertos in ways that differ and that suggests that their criteria was often personal: Ralph Vaughan Williams' Concerto Accademico was founded on 18th century compositional principles; Britten's Concerto Op. 15 is an example of absolute originality regarding form (a second movement *vivace* and a third passacaglia); Somervell's concerto is possibly the most closely tied to the 19th century tradition; Bax's concerto is distinguished for its first movement's particular tripartite division.

They also differ regarding certain technical decisions, such as the presence and position of cadenzas:

Vaughan Williams: only one, in the third movement
Somervell: only one, in the first movement
Box: no cadenza
Britten: an extended cadenza between the second and third movements

They also differ regarding their approaches to the incipts, the quantity of thematic material and metric variety.

And so we come to the conclusion of this book's second part, which together with the first should be considered a kind of introduction to the study of William Walton's Concerto for Violin and Orchestra, the subject that forms the focus of the book.

The treatment provided of the concerto for violin and orchestra in England between 1900 and 193 is brief and does not always go into great detail. It should, however, still permit us to approach a study of Walton and an analysis of his work with an adequate historical-musicological awareness.

PART III

Introduction

In beginning a historical-musicological study of William Walton's Concerto for Violin and Orchestra we first want to delineate the English composer's personal and artistic trajectory. We will set about doing by treating, generically; some of Walton's other works, which constitute the distinctive trail of his musical poetic.

A formal, structural, harmonic and aesthetic analysis of Walton's concerto will allow us to reach the following objectives: identify the concerto's fundamental compositional principles, define the individual character of the Walton's score, and evaluate attentively the composer-performer relationship and the corrections/modifications brought to the score as a consequence of this relationship.

In the appendix we will present some unedited textual material regarding this concerto gathered during research for the book. This material is authored by noteworthy performers and composers who were involved closely or personally with William Walton's music.

William Walton

A professional singer, Charles Walton and a teacher of singing, Louisa Turner, married on August 10th, 1898 in Charlton-cum-Hardy in Manchester. The two then transferred to the city of Oldham, in Lancashire, where Charles became choral director and organist at the church of St. John's Werneth. Over the course of their marriage they had four children: Noel, William, Nora and Alec.

William Turner Walton was born in Oldham on March 29th, 1902 and even from a very young age sang in his father's choir. It was here that he began his musical education: "A special musical talent was early in evidence: his mother reported he could sing phrases from *Messiah* before he could speak."[1]

---

[1] Humphrey Burton & Maureen Murray, *William Walton The Romantic Loner,* 2002, pp.3.

William tried studying the violin without success, and so moved on to the piano, for which he demonstrated a great adeptness.

The birth of two more children, Nora in 1908 and Alec in 1910 put the family at an economic disadvantage. As a result of their difficulties only Noel, the oldest of the four children, was able to attend "grammar school." William was forced study at a local board school.

The youth's future seemed compromised by this misfortune. His luck changed in 1912 when his father read in a local newspaper an advertisement from Oxford University. The Christ Church Cathedral was seeking out young singers. William submitted an application for the audition.

Charles Walton almost ruined William's chances when the night before leaving for Oxford he capriciously blew the money that was to go to William's train ticket: "One can imagine the humiliation Louie Walton must have felt when she discovered that the money for the tickets had all spent on booze. She took over decisively. Cash had to be borrowed from greengrocer."[2]

When William and his mother finally reached Oxford the auditions had terminated. Nevertheless William's mother was able to convince the organist Henry Ley to listen to her son perform Benedetto Marcello's *O Lord our Governor*.

At the age of ten William Walton left his family in Oldham to become a member of Oxford's Christ Church Cathedral School.

The deacon of the Christ Church, Thomas Strong, recognized immediately Walton's musical talent and so followed his education with particular attention (even during the difficult years of World War I). Dr. Walker and Dr. Iliffe were responsable for his education in harmony and counterpoint.

In 1914 William began working on his first compositions, *Variations for Violin and Piano on a chorale by J.S.Bach*, *Choral Fantasia* and *Litany*, using a text by the poet Phineas Fletcher.

Nevertheless it is his *Piano Quartet*, written between 1918 and 1919 and dedicated to deacon Thomas Strong, that is generally considered to be his first work of significant artistic value, "There are echoes in it of Elgar and Frank Bridge as well as the new European masters Ravel and Stravinsky, but the authentic Waltonian voice is already audible, in the romantic sweep of the quartet's melodies, the pungency of its rhythms and the recurring evidence of a musical mind   struggling with formal problems."[3]

---

[2] ivi pp.4.
[3] ivi.pp.22.

During his time in Oxford Walton was in contact with the Sitwell family. In 1920 Walton received an invitation from the Sitwells to move to their London home. Given that he had just abandoned university without attaining a Bachelor of Music Walton was enthusiastic about the opportunity. The three Sitwell siblings, the poetess Edith, the writer Osbert and the art critic Sachervell, had formed an artistic and literary circle that met with figures such as Wilfred Childe, Frank Prewett, Vivian de Sola Pinto and Siegfried Sassoon. And so it was that Walton came to know some of the major players in England's and Europe's literary-musical scene, and developed a capacity for orienting himself in this new and burgeoning artistic and intellectual environment.

Walton took on the title of "adopted or elected brother" of the Sitwells, who offered him opportunities to have intense personal, artistic and cultural experiences that undoubtedly formed part of the composer's adult "education." Together they sojourned in Italy, in 1921. It was the first time that the composer had left the U.K., let alone visited Italy, and Walton was to remain enchanted by the country's beauty.

On returning to England he worked closely with Sitwells on what is considered one of his more successful compositions, *Façade*. The work, completed between November of 1921 and January of 1922, combines the recitation of one of Edith Sitwell's poems, published in 1918 as part of the literary anthology Wheels, with a six instrument accompaniment: flute, clarinet, saxophone, trumpet, cello, percussion. "The music caricatured the popular song, the American fox-trot, and such European dances as the waltz and the polka. It mocked Rossini's The *Barber of Seville*, the Swiss yodel, and Mozart's *Don Giovanni* through parody."[4]

The piece was performed first privately at the Sitwell's home, at 2 Carlyle Square, in Chelsea. A public performance took place on June 12, 1923, in London's Aeolian Hall. Walton returned to work on *Façade's* score in 1927 and then in 1942, only to finalize a definitive version in 1948, for the occasion of its publication.

During the '20s the young composer gradually won recognition in Britain's and Europe's music scene

1923 saw an important step for Walton when the McCullagh Quartet performed his *String Quartet* Op. 1 (written between 1920-1923), for the first International Society of Contemporary Music Festival in Salzburg. In the city Walton met the Austrian composer Alban Berg, who didn't hesitate

---

[4] David Ewen, *The World of Twentieth Century Music*, 1991, pp. 882.

to introduce Walton to his teacher Arnold Schoenberg "an experience from which, happily, he (Walton) emerged with only slight traces of atonalism."[5]

George Gershwin was another composer who Walton had the occasion to know personally and as a result had an influence on Walton's work. Gershwin most certainly formed part of the inspiration for Walton's *Fantasia Concertante,* written between 1923-1924 for two pianos, jazz band and orchestra (incidentally the work was never performed and with Walton's abandoning of jazz the manuscript was destroyed).

In 1926 Walton once again found success at the International Society of Contemporary Music Festival, in Zurich that year, where on June 22nd he presented the orchestral overture *Portsmouth Point.* Walton dedicated the piece to Siegfried Sassoon, one of Walton's more generous financial supporters, "The composition is filled with salty tunes suggesting nautical melodies of eighteenth century and the vigorous rhythms of sailor dances; Constant Lambert also finds the influence of Catalonia sardanas in some of the material." [6]

The same year Walton wrote a composition for chamber orchestra, *Siesta,* dedicated to Stephen Tennant, Sassoon's lover and the Lord and Lady Glenconner's fourth child, who was sick with tuberculosis.

In 1927 Walton returned to work on what had originally been a ballet score, refused by Diaghilev the previous year. Walton developed the work into a composition for orchestra and piano obbligato that he then called the *Sinfonia Concertante.* The work was performed on January 5th, 1928 at London's Queen Hall. Walton dedicated each movement to one of the three Sitwells: the first "To Osbert," the second "To Edith," and the third "To Sachie."

In 1928 he returned to Italy where he composed his Viola Concerto at the Sitwell's winter home on the Amalfi coast. Walton dedicated this work, finished in 1929, to his friend Christabel McLaren. The concerto had been commissioned by the virtuoso Lionel Tertis who then refused to perform it, given the quantity of innovations that the score entailed. It was Paul Hindemith, who Walton had met in Salzburg, who served as the concerto's soloist for the occasion of its first public performance (October 3rd, 1929 at London's Queen's Hall).

The same year the composer received another commission, this time by the BBC, "the first commission ever offered to a composer to write a work specifically for broadcasting."[7]

---

[5] Humphrey Burton & Maureen Murray, *William Walton The Romantic Loner,* 2002, pp.43.

[6] David Ewen, *The World of Twentieth Century Music*, 1991, pp. 883.

[7] Humphrey Burton & Maureen Murray , *William Walton The Romantic Loner,*

The result was *Belshazzar's Feast*, a work for mixed choir, solo baritone and orchestra. The words for the piece were taken from biblical texts, selected by Osbert Sitwell. *Belshazzar's Feast* premiered on October 8th, 1931 at the Leeds Festival, with the London Symphony Orchestra directed by Sir Malcolm Sargent.

So it was that the 29 year old composer, at the beginning of the 1930s, came to be recognized as one of the principal figures of British musical culture. His reputation was helped by early recording techniques, which allowed his works to be heard by a greater audience than was ever before possible.

During these years Walton met his first great love, the baroness Imma von Doernberg, with whom he went to live in Switzerland, in Ascona. Their relationship lasted until 1934, the year in which the baroness abandoned the composer for a Hungarian doctor.

His love for Imma most certainly inspired the first two movements of the symphony that had been commissioned by Hamilton Harty in 1932. But the gradual deterioration of Walton's and Imma's relationship came to pose a growing obstacle in the work's completion. Walton fell into a state of deep depression that was only lifted thanks to the presence of a new figure, the viscount Alice Wimborne, in the composer's life.

Wimborne was the wife of one of the UK's wealthiest men, Ivor Guest, a friend of the Sitwells. A unique personal, intellectual and artistic bond had brought her and Walton together. It was thanks to this bond that Walton's compositional powers were finally renewed.

And so it was that in 1935 the work that had begun 1932 was finally finished. Walton's Symphony No. 1 was performed on November 6th, 1935, at Queen's Hall in London, with great success, "The symphony is a complex work which employs elaborate harmonic and contrapuntal textures and a profusion of terse theme." [8]

Walton had become the most important figure in English music.

The composer's relationship with Alice was not met well by the Sitwells and so after 15 years he decided to leave their residence. During this period Walton worked on scoring films. Among the projects on which he worked were *Escape me never* (1934), *As you like it* (1936) and *Dreaming lips* (1937). The work brought him into contact with well known actors of the day such as Sir Laurence Olivier, with whom Walton struck up a friendship.

2002, pp.62.
[8] David Ewen, *The World of Twentieth Century Music*, 1991, pp.886.

For the occasion of King George VI's coronation Walton was commissioned to write an orchestral march, the *Crown* Imperial. It was performed on May 12th, 1937 at Westminster Abbey during Queen Mary's entrance.

Walton had become officially recognized as England's national composer. In response to such an honour Walton wrote a new cantata for choir and orchestra, *In Honour of the City of London*, dedicated to the Leeds Festival Chorus.

The cantata was composed in 1937 during a sojourn, together with Alice Wimborne, at Villa Cimbrone in Ravello, Italy. It was here that Walton also worked on his Violin Concerto, which we will leave aside for the moment as the work will be treated at great length in the following pages.

The years of World War II saw Walton serving as an ambulance driver for Air Raid Precautions in Warwickshire county. Despite the difficult historical moment Walton continued to dedicate himself to composition. In 1940 he completed his ballet in one act, *The Wise Virgins.* The piece orchestrates selected movements from Bach cantatas (selected and arranged by Walton's friend and colleague Constant Lambert).

That year he received a commission from the Chicago Symphony Orchestra. The offer kept him busy from July to December with the result being the orchestral overture *Scapino.* "In 1941 Walton was called up, only to be exempted from military service in order to compose music for films deemed to be of national importance."[9]

In just 20 days, between December 2nd and 22nd, Walton worked on music for the film *Next of Kin*, with the assistance of Roy Douglas. Immediately after he worked on the music for *Macbeth.* The performance, which took place at the Manchester Opera House in January of 1942, featured the celebrated actor John Gielfud,

Once having joined the Army Film Unit he received a new commission from the BBC, in 1942, to compose the music for the radiophonic comedy *Christopher Columbus.*

That same year he continued to score films, working on *The Foreman Went to France, Went the Day Well?,* and *The First of Few*, from which he extrapolated the orchestral work *Prelude and Fugue: The Spitfire* (from the title of the American version).

In 1943 he worked on the ballet *The Quest,* for the company Sadler's Wells. The following year he worked on the soundtrack for *Henry V,* produced, directed and starring Walton's friend Laurence Olivier.

---

[9] ivi.86.

The war was finally over but it's worth noting that at this point Walton no longer found himself at the center of attention in the world of British music, "while Walton was doing his bit for the war effort and developing a new persona as an Establishment power-broking figure, agreeing to serve on various committees and councils and even putting his name to an impressive blueprint for a future National opera company at Covent Garden, Britten had been composing a string of masterpieces, culminating in his enormously impressive opera *Peter Grimes*, which was mounted at Sadler's Wells in June 1945 only a month after the war in Europe ended."[10]

After completing his *String Quartet* No. 2, first performed on May 5th, 1947 at the Broadcasting House Concert Hall, Walton decided to answer Peter Grimes with an opera of his own.

Encouraged by his companion Alice Wimborne and by yet another BBC commission, the composer dedicated himself in 1947 to the creation of *Troilus and Cressida*, an opera in three acts using Christopher Hassall's libretto. The work progressed slowly in part due to other commissions, such as the music for Oliver's new film, Shakespeare's *Hamlet*. Walton devoted all of 1947 to *Hamlet*.

On April 10 Alice died of lung cancer, despite Walton's desperate efforts at finding the means to finance new medical treatments (that proved to be as ineffective as they were expensive).

After falling into a state of depression, the composer and his painter friend Michael Ayrton left for a long stay

During Walton's first press conference in Buenos Aires he met the woman that was destined to become his future wife, Susana Gil Passo. Shortly after being introduced Walton joked: "You will be very surprised, Miss Gil, to hear that I am going to marry you!"[11]

The young woman, who was working as the British Council's press secretary in Buenos Aires, was surely stunned by Walton's words. She was, however, also charmed by the ways of this eccentric English gentleman who every morning of his stay in the Argentinean capital continued to propose to her. That was until (as Susana recounted)" the conference came to an end, and William was due to return to England. On our last shopping expedition he was silent on the subject of marriage. When I enquired about this change of tactics, he said that, since I had not agreed to marry him, he probably marry one of the girls there who were waiting for his return. I panicked and blurted out, "Please ask me just once more, just try." He did,

---

[10] ivi.87.
[11] Susana Walton, *Behind the Façade,* pp.2.

with a playful grin, because his ruse had worked. Suddenly we were in each other's arms. It was our first kiss, and I was just twenty-two."[12]

A civil marriage was performed in Buenos Aires, on December 18th, 1948. 200 guests (among them four ambassadors) were in attendance for the official ceremony, which took place on January 20th of 1949. "The long estrangement from the Sitwells ended after Lady Wimborne's death and Walton's subsequent marriage."[13]

After a brief stay in London, Walton and his bride decided to leave England to establish a residence in Italy, on the Island of Ischia, where he bought the property Casa Cirillo.

Here he put the finishing touches on the *Violin Sonata*, commissioned by the violinist Yehudi Menuhin in 1947. The work is structured in just two movements: a first in sonata form and a second that is constituted of seven variations.

He also returned to the work of *Troilus and Cressida*, that kept him busy until 1954.

The first performance took place at London's Covent Garden and was received with significant critical and public praise. Cecil Smith wrote in an article that appeared in the Daily Telegraph on December 4th, 1954 that "the first performance of Sir William Walton's "Troilus and Cressida" was the proudest hour for British music since the premiere of Benjamin Britten's "Peter Grimes" nine years ago."

In 1951 the composer was honoured for his commitment to music and England by being knighted, receiving the title Sir William Walton. In 1953 he was again called on to use his talent for England. In that year Elisabeth II was crowned and for the occasion Walton received a commission from the Arts Council. He wrote the coronation march *Orb and Sceptre* and the choral work *Coronation Te Deum* (for two mixed choirs, children's choir, orchestra and military band).

During the '50s Walton continued to receive recognition. He was awarded two honorary doctorates from Cambridge and London University (in addition to one he'd already received from Oxford).

In 1955 he returned to composing music for film with a new work by Olivier, *Richard III*. In 1956 he received a commission from the Johannesburg Festival with the result being the *Johannesburg Festival Overture*. That same year Sir and Lady Walton left Casa Cirillo and moved to another residence, nearby, La Mortella. Hear Susana worked together

---

[12] ivi pp.8.
[13] Humphrey Burton & Maureen Murray, *William Walton The Romantic Loner,* 2002, pp.105.

with the landscape architect Russel Page for the creation an impressive garden, today still considered among the world's most captivating.

At La Mortella the composer worked on the *Cello Concerto*, commissioned by the cellist Gregor Piatigorsky. The concerto's first performance took place at London's Royal Festival Hall in January of 1957 – neither the composer nor his wife were able to assist in the preparations as a minor card accident kept them both in the hospital, "William agonized over a small radio, trying to hear the performance over the air from London, conducted by Malcolm Sargent. Later, tapes were sent him of both the American première and the London performance."[14]

Having recovered from the accident Walton returned to work in the summer of 1957, the project was a commission by the Cleveland Orchestra for their 40th anniversary. Walton wrote the *Partita for Orchestra*, of which he said, "It poses no problems, has no ulterior motives or meaning behind it, and makes no attempt to ponder the imponderable. I have written it in the hope that it may be enjoyed straight off, without any preliminary probing into the score. I have also written it with the wonderful players of the Cleveland Orchestra in mind, hoping that they may enjoy playing it."[15]

The final years of the '50s and the early '60s saw Walton working first on the score of a *Gloria* for the Huddersfield Choral Society and then on his Symphony No. 2, commissioned by and dedicated to the Royal Liverpool Philharmonic Society, "re-dedicated to the memory of George Szell" in 1970.

The work's structure, contrary to his Symphony No. 1 in four movements, is triparted: a first movement, in sonata form, monothematic, a second intensely lyrical movement and a third in the form of a passacaglia, which follows the exposition in octaves of a brief theme with ten variations, a fugue and a coda.

The music critic Peter Heyworth wrote of the work "The usual hallmarks of his music are here – the syncopated rhythmic mannerisms, the rising and falling sevenths that so often recall Elgar, and that strangely bittersweet orchestral palette. If the years have brought any change of emphasis, it is that Walton has come to accept the basically romantic roots of his idiom with increasing frankness."[16]

During the '70s the cold distance that had always existed between the composer and the duo of Britten-Pears began to diminish. Walton's' composition of *Anon in Love* was a testament to this fact. Walton wrote

---

[14] Susana Walton, *Behind the Façade,* pp.166.

[15] William Walton, da *William Walton The Romantic Loner,* 2002, pp.127.

[16] Peter Heyworth, da *The World of Twentieth Century Music*, edited by David Ewen, 1991, pp. 889.

these six songs for tenor and guitar specifically for Peter Pears, who performed the work for the first time in 1960, at the Aldeburgh Festival, with Britten directing.

It was Pears himself who brought up the idea of a musical comedy based on a text by Anton Chekhov. It was on this suggestion that Walton realized his second and final opera, *The Bear, An Extravaganza in One Act* for chamber orchestra and three singers (using Paul Dehn's libretto).

In 1969 Walton paid homage to Britten with the composition for orchestra, *Improvisations on an Impromptu by Benjamin Britten*, founded on a theme from Britten's Piano Concerto.

The composer had already experimented with the scoring of orchestral variations in 1963, with the composition *Variation on a Theme by Hindemith*, inspired by a theme from the second movement of the German composer's Cello Concerto.

Numerous other honours were bestowed on the composer during this period, such as the Freeman Honour, given by birth city of Oldham in 1961, an honorary academic title from the Accademia Nazionale di Santa Cecilia in Rome and the prestigious medal of Order of Merit in 1967.

The composer continued to be productive in this period. For their 125th anniversary the New York Philharmonic commissioned a piece and Walton responded with *Capriccio Burlesco*. Pinewood Studios also asked the composer to author music for the film *The Battle of Britain*. Walton wrote the *Five Bagatelles* between 1970 and 1971 for the British guitarist Julian Bream. The worked was then transcribed with the name *Varii Capricci* for orchestra in honour of the Royal Festival Hall's 25th anniversary.

At the age of 70 the composer who was affectionately called the "Grand Old Man" of English music continued to dedicate himself to his work. Between July and November of 1974 he wrote his brief choral work *Magnificat e Nunc Dimittis*, followed in 1976 by *Roaring Fanfare* and 1977 by *Façade 2, A Further Entertainment*. In 1980 he accepted two commissions by the cellist Mstislav Rostropovich for whom Walton wrote *Passacaglia* for solo cello and *Prologo e Fantasia*, his last composition.

Sir William Walton died on March 8th, 1983 at La Mortella. There his ashes are held under a large rock called "William's Rock." His wife Susana affixed these words by his remains:

SING A SONG OF PRAISE
BELOVED AND REVERED MASTER
THIS ROCK HOLDS HIS ASHES
THE GARDEN HE SURVEYS
RUSSEL PAGE DESIGNED

TOGETHER WE HAPPILY
BROUGHT IT TO LIFE.
SUSANA

"ALL BLISS CONSISTS
IN THIS
TO DO AS ADAM DID"
TRAHERNE 1637-1674

This was the life of William Walton - 80 years of vitality and enthusiasm governed also by reserve and determination. It was this combination that allowed Walton to become one of the greatest English composers of the 20th century and to grow from a "boy from Oldham" into the "grand old man."

The encounters, relationships and events that determined his career were many, the first step being his admission into the Christ Church Cathedral School, where he received his solid foundation in music and musical theory.

Despite his good fortune he was unable to finish his studies at Oxford. But young Walton had the possibility of continuing to grow musically as well as expand both his cultural and personal awareness thanks to one of the most important relationships of his life: his friendship with the Sitwells.

Through them he came to know a great number of the artists, intellectuals and cultural figures of the time: the directors Ernest Ansermet, Sir Thomas Beecham and Eugène Goossens, the music critic Edward Joseph Dent, the painter Walter Sickert, the impresario Diaghilev, the writer Peter Quennell, the novelist Ronald Firbank, the poets Siegfried Sassoon, John Masefield, Wilfred Childe, Frank Prewett and Vivian de Sola Pinto, the composers Constant Lambert, Bernard van Dieren, Peter Warlock, Hyam Greenbaum, Ferruccio Busoni and Vladimir Dukelsky, who in turn introduced Walton to George Gershwin.

With the Sitwells the composer had the possibility of travelling and visiting foreign countries. It was with them that in 1920 he came to know Italy where he decided to return in 1949 for the purpose of establishing a permanent residence.

At the 1923 edition of the International Society of Contemporary Music Walton met Alban Berg, Arnold Schoenberg and Paul Hindemith, with whom he always remained close.

Alongside these great personalities, all of such precious and varying substance, William Walton was able to enrich himself and to develop, even at a young age, an extraordinary maturity and sensibility.

Of course Walton's relationships with the baroness Imma von Doernberg, the viscount Alice Wimborne and the young Argentinian Susana Gil Passo also made their mark on his legacy. At the beginning of the '30s Walton "was well-known in society circles and frequently mentioned by gossip columnist, but his name was never publicly linked with any particular woman until he met the German princess who was to be his first true love: Imma von Doernberg."[17] The relationship, which began in the summer of 1931, was damaged shortly thereafter by their "financial worries and Imma's anxieties, ill health, and intransigence" and finally concluded in 1934.

The years of difficulty that Walton passed with the baroness Imma gave rise to problems with the scoring of the Symphony no. 1's first three movements. It was a symphony that Walton was going to dedicate to his companion.

Walton was unable to complete the work with an adequate finale. It was only thanks to Walton's encounter with the viscount Alice Wimborne that the young composer found the inspiration to complete his symphony "the first fruits of William's and Alice's relationship."[18]

Alice's maturity, culture and balance, let alone wealth, permitted Walton to re-establish himself after his separation from Imma had brought on serious problems with depression and alcoholism. He was finally able to dedicate himself, in an atmosphere of total serenity and comprehension, to the composition of new works, among them his *Violin Concerto*. "A woman who was always important for me ... I was very lucky. Alice Wimborne – so beautiful, intelligent, courteous, brilliant, a great assistant, very musical ... she possessed all the virtues. A wonderful woman."[19]

Alice remained at the composer's side for 13 years, until her death of lung cancer in 1948.

And finally Walton's relationship with Susana Gil Passo, who was destined to become Lady Walton. The energetic and lively Argentinean looked after Walton, supporting him and his work, in which she shared total devotion from the outset.

She never opposed the composer's desire to live in Italy where, in a sort of voluntary exile, the couple spent almost 30 years.

---

[17] Humphrey Burton & Maureen Murray, *William Walton The Romantic Loner*, 2002, pp.45.
[18] Susana Walton, *Behind the Façade*, pp.82.
[19] William Walton, da Tony Palmer, *William Walton: At the Haunted of the Day*. DECCA.

In their residence on Ischia, La Mortella, Susana skilfully and passionately threw herself into the work of creating an enchanting garden "The delight William felt made me see how the boy from Oldham marvelled at having achieved the goal to live and work surrounded by grounds full of flowering bushes and lemon trees. It had been fun to create, and the peace, privacy, and beauty of it made us very proud."[20]

Despite their island residence Walton was never completely isolated. On the contrary he constantly received visitors, friends, composers, musicians such as Samuel Barber, Hans Werner Henze, Thomas Schippers, Gian Carlo Menotti, Spike Hughes, Maria Callas, Lennox Berkeley, Herbert von Karajan, Igor Stravinsky, the actor Laurence Oliver, and the poets Wystan Auden and Chester Kallman and many more.

Also of great importance to his career were his acquaintances with performers, orchestra directors, film and theatre actors, from whom he was always receiving commissions.

He composed for Jascha Heifetz, Gregor Piatigorsky, Yehudi Menuhin, Julian Bream, Mstislav Rostropovich, George Szell, André Kostelanetz, Ernest Irving, Laurence Oliver, the Cleveland Orchestra, the New York Philharmonic, the Chicago Symphony Orchestra, the Royal Liverpool Philharmonic Society and the BBC; he also composed, in honour of their coronation, for King George VI and Queen Elisabeth II, becoming England's "official" national composer.

A colleague once ironically described Walton as "the most mercenary-minded composer I have ever met."[21]

Walton never hesitated to accept a commission – he was quite adept at combining his great skill and personal poetic with the musical tastes and technical needs of those who were requesting the work.

His deep determination pushed him, from a young age, to refine and continually develop his technical ability and ultimately permit him to work adeptly on range of musical forms: symphonic, chamber, operatic, choral, vocal, band, ballets, music for theatre and music for film.

Even at the age of 70 it was with the utmost humility that Walton once again took the opportunity to expand his knowledge of music by accepting a commission by the guitarist Julian Bream: "Never having thought of writing for the guitar, I asked Julian for a chart explaining what the guitar could do."[22]

---

[20] Susana Walton, *Behind the Façade*, pp.176.
[21] Humphrey Burton & Maureen Murray, *William Walton The Romantic Loner,* 2002, pp. 155.
[22] ivi pp.151.

And so we come to understand how Walton's education and trajectory as an artist were absolutely determined by his personal approach to composition.

We also made note of that "conventional" education that began at a young age with his father, then his education at the Christ Church Cathedral School where "he also spent many hours in the Ellis Library in the Radcliffe Camera reading orchestral scores by Debussy, Ravel and Stravinsky"[23] and his unfinished studies at Oxford.

The years spent with Sitwells followed. Osbert Sitwell, one of the three siblings who were so decisive for the composer's maturation and education said "we were able to keep him in touch with the vital works of the age, with the music, for example, of Stravinsky, and to obtain for him, through the kindness of our old family friend [Professor] E.J. Dent, an introduction to Busoni, a modern master of counterpoint [not a fruitful meeting, as it happens: Ferruccio Busoni told his wife that Walton wrote "without imagination or feeling"].... He also had the benefit of consulting Ernest Ansermet on various problems of composition [more likely, conducting]. Moreover by travelling in our company in Italy, Spain and Germany, he soon acquired knowledge of arts, both past and present, belonging to those countries. It was noticeable from the first that he manifested an innate feeling for the masterpieces of painting and architecture, no less than of music: and inevitably the people, landscapes, fiestas and customs he observed increased the store of experience on which he could draw for the enriching of his work."[24]

And so it was that Walton became a composer who was by no means "simple." He understood how to combine the expression of thought with musical feeling, with the expression of a culture and with a broad intellect acquired not just through study but through that "store of experience" to which Osbert makes reference to.

His music was never the product of abstract inspiration or an instinctive propensity towards self-expression. To communicate through musical language was for Walton a deliberate choice, a means to transmit the man's reflections and emotions. Consequently his works are never sophisticated "fables." William Walton chose to write only the authentic chapters of a long autobiography.

---

[23] ivi pp.21.

[24] Osbert Sitwell, da *Laughter in the Next Room*, da *William Walton The Romantic Loner*, 2002, pp. 43.

Violin Concerto

... *sognando* ("dreaming," in Italian)... this is the direction for style and tempo that Sir William Walton gave to the first movement of his Concerto for Violin and Orchestra.

We begin our unpacking of this unusual concerto's historical background by alluding to this exceptionally unusual and intriguing direction.

Sir Walton was thirty four when, one morning in 1936, he entered the Berkeley Hotel in London to be greeted by Jascha Heifetz. "It had been William Primrose, the viola player whom William had met at one of Alice's musical parties, who had suggested to Heifetz to contact William. The viola concerto was by now thought successful, and Heifetz was keen on having a work written especially for him."[25]

The meeting between the two had been organized by a friend of the composer, Spike Hughes, a writer and jazz musician. Hughes later said of the Concerto's inception:

"While William Walton makes his place in the history of English music more certain with every new work, I feel I can claim a tiny share of his success in one instance. Some years ago Jascha Heifetz asked me if I knew a young man by the name of Walton with whom he wanted to discuss a violin concerto. I said I did. Why? Well, could I bring him to lunch. I could and I did, and out of that lunch at the Berkeley (smoked salmon and tournedos) came Jascha's commission for the Walton violin concerto. As a reward for my part in the affair. I have a nicely inscribed score presented "To Spike from William", with the letters written alternatively in red and blue pencil."[26]

The American virtuoso commissioned a concerto for violin from Sir Walton at £300. The composer began to work on the score in January of 1938. In choosing to concentrate on the concerto he abandoned the idea of writing a piece for Benny Goodman and Joseph Szigeti. He also passed on an offer to compose the music for the film *Pygmalion.*

After being operated on for a double hernia in December of 1937, Walton and his companion, the Viscount Alice Wimborne, decided to sojourn on Italy's Amalfi Cost, where for a period they finally settled.

And so it was here that Walton began his work, at Villa Cimbrone in Ravello, a haven for the English (in particular the famous Bloomsbury

---

[25] Susana Walton, *Behind the Façade*, Oxford, Oxford University Press (1988), pp.87.
[26] Spike Hughes, from Neil Tierney, *William Walton: His life and music*, London, Robert Hale (1984), pp.83.

group) on the Amalfi Coast. It was a place frequented by such giants of the times' art, scientific and political communities as Bernard Russel, T.S. Elliot, Virginia Woolf, Winston Churchill, Greta Garbo and Leopold Stokowski.

Here the composer worked, all the while "dreaming," on the first two movements of the Concerto, inspired by the extraordinary beauty of the place in which he found himself and by his intense love for Alice, who encouraged and strongly supported him: "Alice was very good at making him work, and would get very cross when he mucked about."[27]

In addition to the commission for Heifetz, Walton received a proposal by the British Council. The council, through Arthur Bliss, had requested from Walton the score of a violin concerto to present at the New York World's Fair in 1939. Walton wrote to Bliss from Villa Cimbrone in April of 1938:

"The proposal suits me admirably, that is, if everything can be arranged. You may or may not know that Heifetz has commissioned me to write a violin concerto and I have just got started on it. The only question is if he will agree to the first performance being under the auspices of the British Council. I think he probably will do as it seems to me as good a first performance platform as he will ever get. My terms with him are that he pays me a certain sum for the right to be the sole performer for a certain length of time. I don't know if the British Council would insist on a British violinist appearing in New York – if so I am afraid it would dish the whole thing, or at any rate I should have to decide whether Heifetz or the British Council took it. But it is obvious that the best arrangement would be for the "world première" to be played by Heifetz under the auspices of the British Council."[28]

In May of the same year Walton wrote to editor Hubert Foss of the commission. The letter revealed some concerns:

"I replied in the affirmative, stipulating that Heifetz should play first performance. The British Council's terms not clashing with Heifetz's, I could try and kill two birds with one stone, for he can do whatever he likes about the work after the first performance.... What, however, seems to be the greatest drawback is the nature of the work itself. It seems to be developing in an extremely intimate way, not much show, bravura, and I begin to have doubts (fatal for the work, of course) of this small voice getting over at all in a vast hall holding ten thousand of people."[29]

---

[27] ibidem.
[28] William Walton, from *The Selected Letters of William Walton*, London, Faber & Faber (2002), pp.113.
[29] ivi pp.114.

In summer of 1938 the composer returned to London where he presented the first two movements of the work to the Spanish violinist Antonio Brosa from whom he received some suggestions for improving the part of the solo violin. Brosa wrote of his contribution:

"I asked Walton if he had written anything for the violin and he told me he was writing a concerto for Heifetz and I said : 'Oh, that is very interesting. May I see the concerto, please? Would you show it to me?' And he said: 'Well, yes, I could, but as matter of fact I am very fed up because I do not know very well how to write for the violin,' and I said: ' Well, nowadays you know very well how to write for the violin,' and so eventually he had a copy made. He had written two movements, the first and the second, and he lent it to me and I practiced it, and he came home and played it with me and I made a few suggestions and so on."[30]

Collaborating with Brosa failed to entirely assuage Walton:

"Mrs. Dora Foss wrote to her husband, then in America, in January 1939 informing him that Walton, clearly in a very troubled frame of mind, had telephoned her from Rugby [where he had been staying at the residence of Alice Wimborne] to say, 'I am having great difficulty in making the last movement elaborate enough for Heifetz to play it.' She also reported that, during an hour-long conversation, he had expressed the fear that Heifetz would not, after all, play the new work when it was completed and felt perhaps he ought to ask Kreisler to play... Attempting to cheer him up, Mrs. Foss said of the concerto, 'anyhow, I'm sure it's better than anyone else could write' (or something similar), to which, with a characteristic, breezy self-esteem, he answered, 'Oh, I've no doubt about that!' "[31]

The composer, despite the difficulties he'd been having, was able to produce a rough draft of the third movement and sent a complete copy of the manuscript to Heifetz. The American violinist replied by telegram on February 28th 1939:

"Accept enthusiastically your concerto however collaboration necessary please advise earliest possible date you arrival letter follows greetings Heifetz."[32]

---

[30] *A Conversation with Antonio Brosa*, Royal College of Music Magazine, London, Easter (1969), pp.10.

[31] Neil Tierney, *William Walton: His life and music*, London, Robert Hale (1984), pp. 85.

[32] from Humprey Burton and Maureen Murray, *William Walton The Romantic Loner*, Oxford, Oxford University Press (2002), pp.83.

The virtuoso Heifetz was confused as to the directions given by his Spanish colleague and invited the composer to come to the U.S. to work on the score. "Walton was angry and upset. 'For tuppence I would give it to you' he said to Brosa. 'I am not like Heifetz' said the other. 'He can play it anywhere he likes. He can make records, I cannot.' "[33]

In March of that year Walton wrote to the orchestra director Leslie Heward to inform him of his disengagement from the British Council commission:

"As you may have seen I've withdrawn my Concerto from World's Fair not as is stated because it's unfinished but because Heifetz can't play on the date fixed (the B.C. only let him know about ten days ago!) Heifetz wants the concerto for two years and I would rather stick to him. But actually I'm afraid there is little to be said for either the British Council or myself, so keep this 'under your hat'. So I'm out of the World's Fair altogether. I understand that all the music programmes barring those of the B.C. have been cancelled and that nothing is happening at all. Unfortunately I know very little about American conditions, but I am going over sometime soon to work with Heifetz on the concerto probably the same time as you..."[34]

In May of 1939 the composer, together with companion Alice, left for America on board the transatlantic SS Normandy. Years later Walton described the meeting with Heifetz to his wife Susana: "He didn't even play the piece through, although he did later jazz up the last movement a bit."[35]

After three weeks of work the score was finished. Later Walton said of June 2nd 1939 "as I was leaving the question of being paid arose. Was it £ 200 or $1,500? I said £ 300, not realizing by then that the pound was a bit shakey even those days. So he took out a bit of paper, rang up his bank and gave me $ 1,493 and some cents! He'd made on the deal!"[36]

Just before heading back to Europe, Walton granted an interview to the New York Times in which he declared "today's white hope is tomorrow's black sheep. These days it is very sad for a composer to grow old- unless,

[33] ibidem.

[34] William Walton from Susana Walton, *Behind the Façade*, Oxford, Oxford University Press (1988), pp.91.

[35] ivi pp.91.

[36] Osbert Sitwell, *Laughter in the Next Room,* da Humprey Burton and Maureen Murray, *William Walton The Romantic Loner*, Oxford, Oxford University Press (2002), pp.83.

that is, he grows old enough to witness a revival of his work. I seriously advise all sensitive composers to die at the age of 37. [His age exactly] I know: I've gone through the first halcyon periods, and am just ripe for my critical damnation."[37]

In a letter, dated October 15th 1939, the composer wrote to Heifetz to inform the violinist that he would be unable to assist in the first performance of the concerto, which had been planned for December of that year in Cleveland. World War II had just broken out and Walton had been enlisted to drive ambulances for Air Raid Precautions.

Reproduced here is part of that historical letter[38]:

Ashby St. Ledgers
Rugby
Oct. 15th 1939

Dear Heifetz,

Thank you for your letter, since receiving it I have heard from Mr. Foss that the first performance is to be at Cleveland on Dec 7th & 9th, and I am delighted about it. Alas, I don't think owing to this something war, there is the slightest likelihood of my being able to get over for it, what with the difficulties of travel & the difficulty of not only the expense, of obtaining any dollars, also I'm of military age and am liable to be called up, but when, the powers that be (there are too many of them!) will decide.

Meanwhile I have become an ambulance driver for the local A.R.P. though I must admit that it dosent (sic) entail much, as everything, as you will have read in the papers, has been very quiet as regards air raids. In fact, this is a peculiar war & not working out as predicted & it looks as if the side that can bore the other most, will win.

Music, as you can imagine, was killed stone dead at the outset, & the BBC have hardly, with rare exceptions, broadcast a decent piece of music since war started. Why? Noone (sic) will ever know!

However, things are looking up a bit, & some concerts are going to be given soon, chiefly in the provinces.

This state of thing, I need hardly say, is having a disastrous affect (sic) on composers & players, who depend on music for their income. So what with the income tax at 7/6 in the £ (and 17/6 for the rich), things are not

---

[37] Neil Tierney, *William Walton: His life and music*, London, Robert Hale (1984), pp. 86.
[38] This unpublished letter was found in the archives of the William Walton foundation in Ischia. To (the best of) my knowledge this is the first time it has been used in any analysis of Walton's work.

exactly rosy, but I suppose that is what one has to sacrifice for allowing a lunatic to take charge of Europe, or at least try to.

Is the concerto going to be broadcast? If so, could you be so kind as to let me know the time & wavelength. Also if it is, could you have a record taken of it "over the air" & send it to me as it seems to me to be the only way I shall have, or may ever have, of hearing the work, at any rate for a very long time. I think I should have no real difficulty in being allowed to buy enough dollars to pay for them.

The letter then proceeds with an interesting listing of the various corrections that Walton had made to the score. This will be treated later with greater depth.

The première went off on December 7th of 1939, at the Severance Hall of Cleveland, Ohio, with the Cleveland Orchestra directed by Artur Rodzinksi.

While the "small voice", which had so concerned Sir Walton, was lifted through Severance Hall by the violin of Jascha Heifetz the composer was, in fact, on the other side of the ocean driving an ambulance under a hail of enemy bombs.

Heifetz reported back to Walton by way of a telegram dated December 8th, 1939: "Concerto enormous success orchestra played superbly you would have been extremely pleased congratulations your most successful concerto writing sending program best greetings thanks Jascha Heifetz"[39]

The extraordinary critical and public reception was amply recounted the following day, also by the newspapers. Arthur Loesser wrote an article entitled 'Praises Heifetz, Rodzinski in pioneer concerto': "It is a true violin concerto, with the solo instrument taking the lead almost everywhere... The orchestral portion of the concerto was most skillfully and discreetly handled by Dr. Artur Rodzinski. To say that the solo part was played with superlative brilliance and understanding, and with unapproachable mastery of bow and fingers, is merely a long-wide way of saying that it was played by Jascha Heifetz."[40]

Elmore Bacon, with the article 'Heifetz wins ovation for concerto,' declared "Jascha Heifetz, Dr. Artur Rodzinski and the Cleveland Orchestra were given a stirring ovation after the world premiere of William Walton's new concerto at Severance Hall last night. An overflow audience was clamorous in its reception of this new addition to the violin repertoire. The

[39] from Humprey Burton e Maureen Murray, *William Walton The Romantic Loner*, Oxford, Oxford University Press (2002), pp.83.
[40] Arthur Loesser from Herbert-Axelrod Heifetz, Neptune City, NJ, Paganiniana (1976), pp.375.

demonstration was further heightened by Heifetz insisting upon the orchestra standing with him to share in the acclaim."[41]

News of the triumph got to England quickly where a newspaper in Oldham (Walton's birthplace) reported in an article with the headline "William Walton's new concerto: ambulance work keeps him from premiere" the following of Rodiz,nski, the concerto's director "Mr. Arthur Rodiznski, conductor of the orchestra, said that the concerto was absolutely one of the finest violin concertos ever written'."[42]

The first performance in the U.K. was announced for February of 1941 and was to take place at the Sheldonian Theatre of Oxford, in occasion of the conferring of an honorary doctorate on the composer.

Due to bombardments that effected also the composer's house in South Eaton Place, Walton's original score was lost during the war; Heifetz's copy, with its detailed notes, was photocopied in New York, as a precaution, and then sent to Oxford University Press in London. During its voyage to England this original was also lost (due to a naval accident on the Atlantic).

As a result Walton had to wait until November 1st 1941, to present his concerto to his home country. The performance took place in the Royal Albert Hall of London with the London Philharmonic Orchestra (breaking from the original idea of a performance at Oxford). Henry Holst served as the soloist.

> "A gramophone recording of the concerto, performed by Heifetz, also went down with his proofs. Since neither Walton nor Holst had previously heard the work played, they had no interpretative signposts to guide them. Moreover, according to Malcolm Arnold, who played trumpet in the London Philharmonic Orchestra, the first printed score contained so many incredible errors that he felt sure it was 'junked' and regarded his own copy of the score as 'a curiosity to be prized'."[43]

In 1943 the composer returned to work on the score of the concerto. A letter dated December 23 recounts:

> " ...I've been taking the opportunity during a lull in Henry V to rescore the Vl. Con. I started out to do a little patching here & there but found it not a

---

[41] ivi pp.376.

[42] from Humprey Burton e Maureen Murray, *William Walton The Romantic Loner*, Oxford, Oxford University Press (2002), pp.88.

[43] from Neil Tierney, *William Walton: His life and music*, London, Robert Hale (1984), pp. 87.

satisfactory way of doing it, so more or less I started from the beginning &
I have even gone as far as to introduce a bass clarinet! On:

Instead of the timp. I sent it to be copied next week in the hope the parts
will be ready for a performance at Birmingham on Jan 17th . If they are
ready you must come down & hear it. I think now that I've got it as good
as I can get it."[44]

On January 17th 1944 a revisited version of the concerto was
performed at the Civic Hall of Wolverhampton, again with Holst as the
soloist and now with the Liverpool Philharmonic Orchestra supporting
him. Sir Malcolm Sargent served as director for this new version which
saw, in part, elaborations in terms of orchestral range and timbre.

The two founding spirits of the concerto, Walton and Heifetz, met
again in London, in June of 1950, for the RCA recording of the work. It
was an accomplishment that called to an end the collaboration that began
at the Berkley Hotel in 1936 between the American violist and his British
counterpart.

A new recording of the concerto was made with violinist Yehudi
Menuhin and the London Symphony Orchestra, directed by Walton
himself, in July of 1969 at Abbey Road Studios (EMI) in London. The
composer wrote shortly thereafter from his garden, la Mortella, in the bay
of Naples:

---

[44] William Walton from *The Selected Letters of William Walton*, London, Faber &
Faber (2002), pp.147.

Dear Yehudi,

>After my few days recording in London I returned here with our recording of the Concertos. [The Violin and Viola Concertos: Menuhin played solo parts of both]
>Your playing is absolutely astounding, in fact I am unable to conjure up adequate superlatives for your interpretation & performance- nor can I thank you enough for having brought to life a dream which I thought would never come true.[45]

This is the background for Sir William Walton's Violin Concerto, written during some of the most significant years of the composer's life. These were years that traversed his meeting and getting to know Heifetz, his love for Alice, his travels in Italy and America and the outbreak of World War II.

Undoubtedly the score reflects and channels various "geographic" influences: England (with its nostalgic lyricism in the style of Sir Edward Elgar), America (felt by Jascha Heifetz's "jazz" contribution) and, of course, Italy, with the strong Mediterranean shades that pervade the entire concerto.

Sir Walton's deep intellectual and emotional bond with Alice Wimborne fed the romantic and lyrical identity of the concerto while the emphasis on virtuosity and technical achievement, explored through the technical and expressive possibilities of the solo violin, derived from his association with Jascha Heifetz. This was a relationship born in that twentieth century custom by which a master commissioned a concerto from a specific composer.

For the rest of his life Walton remained deeply tied to this work. In April of 1982, less than a year before his death, he participated in a BBC radio program called 'Desert Island Discs', "during which the 'castaway' is invited to choose the eight records he would like to hear on his desert Island."[46]

Walton had no doubts – on a desert island he would have brought along also a copy of his own Violin Concerto.

---

[45] ivi pp. 389.
[46] Susana Walton, *Behind the Façade*, Oxford, Oxford University Press (1988), pp.239.

It is now time to move to an analysis of the score of the concerto. We must remember that there remain two autograph manuscripts of the score: a reduced version for violin and piano dated May 15, 1939 (New York), kept at Washington's Library of Congress, and the complete score of the revisited version from 1943, belonging to the collection of Frederick R. Koch, kept at the Beinecke Rare Book and Manuscript Library at Yale University.

This analysis is based on the second manuscript, utilized by Oxford University Press for the 1945 publication of the concerto's score, reprinted in 1952 and corrected in 1969.

The composition of the orchestra is as follows:

2 flutes, 1 piccolo, 2 oboes, 1 English horn, 2 clarinets (in A), 2 bassoons, 4 horns (in F), 2 trumpets in Bb, 2 trumpets, 3 trombones, timpani, percussion (snare drum, xylophone, cymbals, tambourine), harp, strings.

The original differs only for the presence of a glockenspiel, gong, bass drum and castanets.

First movement. *Andante tranquillo*

In the first three pages of the manuscript kept at Beinecke Library we find notes, written by Walton himself, for the first and third movements. The first of these notes reads: "A part [sic?] the accompanying motif ,the 1st subject consists? of two themes : the main one on the solo Vl. and its counter on the Fg. Thesis."

In the absence of a full orchestral opening the concerto commences on a B minor chord, ppp, played by horns, double basses and snare rolls. The first clarinet and then the violas play "the accompanying motif," I C. The last beat of the second measure follows with the solo violin's entrance, which, *sognando*, expounds "the main theme" of the first subject, I A.

At this point the counterpoint of the third measure begins, played *espressivo* by bassoons and violoncellos, I B. "The opening leap is naturally an octave to strengthen the effect of anacrusis, but the interval that gives its character to the melody is the seventh, as can be observed not only in the second and third occurrences of this significant leap, but elsewhere between the pivot notes of the swaying tune."[47]

---

[47] Frank Howes, *The Music of William Walton*, Oxford, Oxford University Press.

We notice a significant amount/number of expressive markings, in particular the marks for crescendo and diminuendo. We also notice the indication, given twice, "*sognando*," for the solo violin and *espressivo* for bassoons, violas and violoncellos. As Yehudi Menuhin remembers, many of these notes were added by Heifetz as well " ...edited by him, bears witness to the minuteness of his planning, indicating expressive marks in unusual detail, in crescendi and diminuendi on single notes. He strove for a control so complete that each performance would be identical."[48]

In January of 1947 Kenneth Avery wrote an interesting article for the musicological journal **Music and Letters**, in which he suggests that the first subject represents an "unconscious quotation from the composer's

---

(1947), pp.61.

[48] Yehudi Menuhin, *Unfinished Journey*, London, Macdonald & Jane's (1997), pp. 158.

song *'Daphne'*."[49] *Daphne* is the first of the *Three Songs* for voice and piano written by Walton between 1931 and 1932. This work sets a text by Edith Sitwell.

After comparing the two scores we realize how much Avery's impression is solely a personal one on his part. Indeed it seems difficult to locate a real similarity between the subjects of the two works. It seems advisable to discard this idea of an "unconscious quotation."

Here is the the the subject of ***Daphne***:

Returning now to the concerto, the exposition of the first subject, constituted of two simultaneous lyrical melodies, is accomplished according to the parameters of sonata form, in 16 measures, concluding on the dominant. A 24-measure modulating bridge follows. This moves across four harmonic progressions of semitones from the key of B minor to that of Eb minor. In his manuscript Walton indicated "from here [measure 16, the end of the exposition of the first subject] on to No 5 is elaborated restatement".

An orchestral tutti then introduces the second subject, II A, a *cantabile espressivo* played by first violins, violas, flutes and oboes in unison, accompanied by quatrains in the harp and sextuplets in the clarinets.

II A

A modulation announces the new entrance of the solo violin, at number 6, marked in the manuscript *risoluto* and *quasi improvvisando* (in the printed OUP edition this indication is not present). We notice a strong resemblance between the descending sextuplet pattern of the 54th measure, the third measure of number 6 and the descending triplet and quadruplet patterns of the 23rd measure of the second movement of Elgar's Violin Concerto. In fact the two passages, seen below, share a similar rhythmic design and the same notes (except for a difference of semitones in Bb and Eb in Elgar).

---

[49] Kenneth Avery, *Music and Letters*, ML ,vol. xxviii no.1 (1947), pp. 8.

Walton

Elgar

Walton wrote: " till 7 the solo Vl. discourses on the 1st four bars (19-22) of the 2nd sub.; at 7 there is a restatement of 2nd sub, a fragment of I A (bar 3) (first on the ob. then on diminution on the Cl.) being introduced at the 4th bar after 7"

Number 8 follows with a change in tempo, from 4/4 to 12/8, in which the solo violin plays chords on 2, 3 and 4 strings re-elaborating a part of the material of the first subject, I A, and moves with a wide rallentando towards the development; "at 8 a short reference to I A (9-10-11) is made, but varied rhythmically leading to the development which takes place between 9 e 15".

The development opens in the key of F minor with a rhythmic variation of subject I A (that we will call I D), executed by the woodwinds and accompanied by a rush of quatrains of semiquavers, played by the strings.

Walton confirmed: "I A (1 -7) but varied on rhythm texture a pace (E = 184)".

I D

The solo violin then enters, first playing I D a semitone above, in unison with the first oboe, and then a long episode of semiquaver quatrains, played *ff veloce strepitoso*, moves towards the cadenza.

I B is recapitulated by two solo trombones in 11 and in 12 by flutes, oboes, clarinets and trumpets while I A is recapitulated 4 measures before 13 by the first trumpet and at 13 by flutes, oboes, clarinets and trombones.

Walton wrote "At 11 it is based on I B (2-7) the same at 12 bit in diminution. 4 bars before 13 I A (1-3) appears and again cit 13 by now properly distorted and the cadenza begins at 5 after 13 based on I A (6-7)".

After a rapid descending scale, a long trill, *agitato*, 3rd and 2nd chords and new trills, the solo violin conclude the cadenza, moving into the key of G minor.

And so the movement proceeds with a now augmented second subject, II A, in *p sonore espressivo*, accompanied "by a conventionalized five-note figure derived from the opening of I A over an 'um-pum-pum bass' ".[50]

I E

At number 18 the solo violinist recapitulates I A in a high register. It is then silent from number 19 until shortly before 22, during which time the orchestra re-elaborates the thematic material of I B.

These are the composer's notes, present in the manuscript:

"The cadenza leads to the return of the 2nd sub No.5 (what you – [here it is impossible to determine what Walton was referring to]- refer to as the episode in g min) but it's not a return being in augmentation on the solo Vl. While the accompaniment is made up from fragments from I A. At 18 there is a reference to the passage between 8 and 9 leading to a further development based again on I B and I A. At 20 I B (16-17-18) of not much account begins to emerge and to a certain extant predominates to the end of the movement. The re-entrance of the solo (5 after 21) is based on this passage which leads to the recapitulation of the 1st sub. At 22."

[50] Frank Howes, *The Music of William Walton*, Oxford, Oxford University Press (1947), pp.66.

The repetition begins with another entrance by the soloist now three measures before number 22. The entrance features theme an exposition of I B, while two solo flutes repeat I A (at the movement's beginning the solo violin played I A). Sixteen measures after number 22 the soloist re-appropriates the theme I A and the bassoons play their "accompanying motif" I C, whose rhythm is now pronounced by timpani *coperti e col legno* and by the harp *staccato secco*. The two flutes alternate in the performance of the pattern I E and the English horn recapitulates I B. From number 24 on the flutes and bassoons alternate with the descending pattern I E.

I E

Walton wrote again in his manuscript: "This time the orchestra takes I A and the solo I B . At 24 the figure No.4 (I E) based on I B (16-17-18) appears again in conjunction with I A (1-5) and I B (2-7)   (this passage actually is at 5 after 24)"

Ten measures from the end, number 26, basses and the second bassoon return for a light exposition of the second subject, II A, which is then repeated an octave above by violas and clarinets. The solo violin concludes with harmonic thirds in the key of B minor, sustained by the harmonics of two solo violas, *colla parte*, and by pizzicatos by violins, violoncellos and contrabasses. "At 26 there is a reference to the 2nd sub. 5 a bit scanty I'll admit but sufficient I trust, to recall it." The following represent the last directions Walton left in the concerto's manuscript:

"Actually the form of this movement is more a matter of 'weights + measures' than strict ordinary 'sonata' form, in fact to put it into sections it works out roughly, like this

From the beginning to 5 is balanced by the section from 22 to end

From 5 to 22 could be called the middle section in its tun (?) has its own balancing , pivoting on the cadenza

5 to 9	is balanced by	15 to 19
9 to 15	is balanced by	19 to 22

which may be an odd and obscure way of working out form."

None of the studies that were researched made reference to the manuscript held at the Beinecke Rare Book and Manuscript Library at Yale University. And yet here the composer clearly affirms not having adopted for the first movement the principles of the traditional sonata form.

Despite the desire by scholars to invoke the sonata form during analysis, given Walton's admission that he did not consider it a basis for his work, it is felt that in this case such an analysis would be inexact and unnecessary. It was as if Walton himself was advising those who would later come to study his work that it would be "odd and obscure" to schematize his concerto according to the parameters of the traditional sonata form.

In fact the development section is notably more extended with respect to the exposition and the recapitulation. Moreover in this last section the second subject is not distinctly re-exhibited but reemerges only a few measures before the end.

Robert Meikle observes, to that end, that " the dimensions of many movements in Walton's symphonies and concertos are such that any investigation of them cannot but explore their relationship to sonata form, and it at once becomes clear that if, in the symphonies, Walton relies on the more orthodox dimensions of sonata structure, in the concertos he seizes the advantage offered by the presence of the solo instrument to expand and explore its potential."[51]

Second Movement. *Presto capriccioso alla napoletana*

Walton wrote to his editor, Hubert Foss, in 1938 from Villa Cimbrone: "Having been bitten by a tarantula a rare & dangerous & unpleasant experience I have celebrated the occasion by the 2nd movement being a kind of tarantella 'Presto capricciosamente alla napolitana'. Quite gaga I may say & of doubtful propriety after the 1st movement- however you will be able to judge."[52]

The second movement, a Scherzo, opens with the exposition of I A by the orchestra, which is followed by the soloist's entrace with I B's pattern of quintuplets and triplets. "Tonality is not quite so straightforward, since

[51] Robert Meikle, da Stewart R. Craggs, *William Walton: Music and Literature*, Aldershot, Ashgate Publishing (1999),pp. 75.
[52] from Stephen Loyd, *William Walton : Muse of Fire*, Rochester, NY, Boydell Press (2001), pp.168.

the main theme is characterized by interval of the augmented fifth, which is subversive of key."[53]

I A

I B

From the tenth measure, number 27, the orchestra participates together with the violin soloist in the "tarantella," as Walton marked clearly in the manuscript.

From number 29, *giocoso leggiero*, while the solo violin alternates harmonic triplets with triplets pizzicato, the first violins play theme I C (whose origins clearly lie in Neapolitan folk music) together with the flute and piccolo.

After eight measures, number 30, strings, horns, clarinets, English horn and bassoons interject with I D, which only momentarily interrupts the soloist's "danza."

I C

[53] Frank Howes, *The Music of William Walton*, Oxford, Oxford University Press (1947), pp. 67.

I D

A tutti again interrupts the soloist with a rhythmic variation on I D. A change in tempo follows, from 2/2 to 3/4, along with soloist's exposition of a waltz theme, in intervals of sixths, accompanied by pizzicatos by strings, the harp and muted horns.

I E

The return to 2/2 time marks the new orchestral exposition of I A and the presence, again, of the soloist who performs now variations on I B. The woodwinds then interrupt the soloist, twice expounding I F from 35.

I F

At this point, number 36, Walton inserts a Trio section (Canzonetta), beginning with the two horns' theme, I G. The solo violin wedges itself between the various solos by the horns, the clarinets, the English horn and violoncellos, repeating a pattern of triplets similar to "a Chopinesque spiral thread",[54] I H. The soloist then goes on to a trill on a high G for the brief affirmation, I L.

---

[54] Franck Merrick, *Walton's Concerto for Violin and Orchestra*, *The Music Review No.2* (1941), pp.309-18.

I G

I H

I L

A double execution of theme I G, played by the solo violin, follows for the four measures after 39. The second execution is played up an octave using dreamy harmonics. 40 proceeds with a variation on two strings of what has just been played. This is accomplished at first at with thirds and then at different intervals.

From the 8th measure of 41 clarinets, oboes and flutes play I H and the solo violin, above the murmuring of rolling timpani, moves towards the close of the Trio with a pattern of thirds.

At number 42 the Scherzo begins again with a new orchestral exposition of theme IA. This is followed by the violin's entrance in the new tempo 4/4, alternating, at times, with 2/4, 3/8 and 5/8.

At 44 a new tutti comes forth with a rhythmic variation of I D, after which the solo violin resumes its virtuosistic course, that is until number 48 when it returns to play the waltz theme I E, *lontano* (omitted in the OUP edition). The violoncellos echo in *pp espressivo* the theme, I G, of the Trio.

A sudden return of tempo I signals the conclusion of the movement, with the solo violin playing, again, the original pattern I B.

The second movement is certainly that which was most influenced by Walton's relationship to Italy. The tarantella and the section of Trio Canzonetta, by which the concerto acquires its "Mediterranean" character, are a clear testimony to Walton's deep awareness of traditional Neapolitan folk music. The movement is distinct, above all, for its absolute technical difficulty, for which the composer spent a long time and exerted great energy.

Walton, who possessed only a minimal capacity for playing the violin and had never composed a work for solo violin before the concerto, found himself writing for the greatest virtuoso of the moment, Jascha Heifetz.

His continual concern that he would be unable to satisfy the needs of a musician who had requested a work worthy of his extraordinary musical skill, is therefore understandable.

Yet despite the difficulty Walton succeeded in putting forth a complex violin score, capable of combining technical virtuosity with intense emotion."The whole movement gives the soloist an opportunity for hair-raising virtuosity, from rapid arpeggios and spectral harmonics to languid parallel sixths, double-stopped trills and, in the trio, a stratospheric cantabile, again on harmonics. No wonder Heifetz was reported as being 'very crazy about it'."[55]

Third Movement. *Vivace*

The final movement opens with an exposition, without accompaniment, of the staccato march theme, I A, played by bassoons, violoncellos and contrabasses in pp for fifteen measures. " The key is B major: the first phrase outlines a stepwise ascent from B to its dominant, F # , and the ensuing measures confirm the tonality with a chromatic descent in the (implied) upper voice and a dominant-tonic cadence in the bass."[56]

I A

The solo violin then enters, at number 50, reiterating the theme I A on two strings and with chords, "while chords on the horns and pizzicato

---

[55] Robert Meikle, da Stewart R. Craggs, *William Walton: Music and Literature*, Aldershot, Ashgate Publishing (1999), pp.94.
[56] Anne Marie de Zeeuw, *Tonality and the Concertos of William Walton*, U. of Texas, Austin, (1983), pp. 226.

strings emphasize the fact that there is to be no question of a fugue."[57] At number 52, *molto animato*, strings and woodwinds exhibit the second principal theme, I B, after which the solo violin presents the intensely lyrical 2nd subject, II A.

I B

Walton wrote in his manuscript, " The exposition consist of 2 themes. I B leading to 2nd subject which takes longer than it might appear on paper 1-20 which may be too long for a melody which hardly repeats itself?"

II A

Walton continued to write, next to example II A, "I discovered an unconscious quotation from the Viola Con. in the 5th   bar (of the 2nd subject)." Number 55 marks the beginning of the development. First the orchestra recalls I A and then the solo violin re-elaborates I B, accompanied by pizzicatos on the strings, bassoons and clarinets. This leads into a new orchestral exposition of I B (at number 57) and five measures later the return of I A.

The composer's notes confirm: "The development begins promptly at 55 restating I A immediately followed by an extended version of I B."

Beginning with number 59 the two themes, I A and I B, combine in a series of simultaneous entrances (by bassoons, oboes and flutes playing I A and violas and solo violin playing I B) until number 60, when the solo violin presents a new version, augmented, of I B *grazioso* (not *sognando* as improperly indicated in the OUP version), accompanied by a version, in diminution, of A (bassoons and cellos) and of B (clarinets).

---

[57] Franck Merrick, *Walton's Concerto for Violin and Orchestra*, *The Music Review No. 2* (1941), pp. 315.

"At 59 I A and I B are worked in conjunction with one another till at 60 an augmented version of I B blossoms forth with fragments of I A and I B in diminution serving as accompaniment"

After that which Walton called a "short cadenza," at number 62, the orchestra briefly reaffirms I B (following a short solo on oboe and clarinet). Above them the solo violin twice performs jumping 7ths (recalling the octaves of the initial measures of the concerto) and a long trill, moving towards a new exposition of the second subject, II A, this time played by the first oboe and the first clarinet. The composer indicated: "After a short cadenza 62 the return of the 2nd sub. II appears at 64 this time with the melody in the orchestra while the [violin] descants with a version of I A"

Number 66 follows with a recapitulation, with bassoons and cellos again expounding the initial theme I A, in the dominant tone. From number 67 the solo violin presents a new, augmented version of I A, now in the original key, accompanied by cellos and violas in a version that is in diminution.

A long tutti from number 69 to 73 combines and elaborates the thematic fragments of I A and I B, as reported in the manuscript: "The tutti commences at 69 being a more savage version of the passage between 59 and 63".

Introduced by rolling timpani, pulsing strings, cellos played pizzicato and a pattern of fifths F#, B, E repeated by the harp, the violin soloist returns to exhibit *arditamente* (omitted in the OUP edition) the first theme of the first movement, I A, at the 4th measure of number 73. The version is augmented and played on two strings in intervals of sixths .

From the ninth measure of 73 bassoons, clarinets and English horn accompany the solo violin for theme I A of the third movement. The second measure of number 75 begins the accompanied cadenza. This development is marked by a change from 3/4 time to 4/2 that in turn transforms into a *sognando con molto espress* in 12/4.

Walton described this section as follows: "At 73 above a rolling pedal derived from 66 the solo enters with an augmented version of the 1st theme from the 1st mov. At the 9th bar after 73 it is accompanied by fragments of I A so coordination between the themes becomes more apparent . This leads to the cadenza which is ....?..... from the 2nd sub. II and I A the double 1st sub. of the 1st mov."

The long cadenza concludes at number 81 where basses and cellos *deliberatamente* initiate the coda with a new exposition of the staccato theme I A.

A new rhythmic change, from 3/4 to 2/2 signals the entrance of the solo violin that with a pattern of thirds moves in crescendo towards the episode, *Alla Marcia* at number 82. The composer wrote in the manuscript (and in a letter to Heifetz that will be reproduced later) during his military call up: "The coda starts off with I A, with the time signature ultimately changing to 2/2; when I A emerges as a march (the 'conscription') at 82 snatches of I B appear, at 83 the whole is rounded off by an augmentation of I A at 84."

The orchestra accompanies the violinist's virtuosistic part with a re-elaboration, at number 83, of the theme I B and at number 84 of the theme I A in a finale that is rhythmically energetic and vibrant and which concludes in the key of B major.

Having the possibility to view and analyze a piece of music's original manuscript contributes, undoubtedly, to our capacity to understand "up close" the principles and compositional mechanisms that regulate the work. It is therefore one of the fundamental keys to producing an effective study, especially in this case where we find attached to the manuscript an explanation by the composer himself.

It is a surprise then that none of the previous analyses conducted on Walton's Violin Concerto is based on the original manuscript kept at Yale's Beinecke Rare Book and Manuscript Library (except perhaps Franck Merrick's which, nevertheless, never makes explicit reference to the manuscript).

Beyond containing a concise analysis of the first and third movements, conducted by Walton himself, the manuscript allows us to gather, by way of an exceptional quantity of notes and directions, the original intentions of the composer.

Scholars don't have to limit themselves to an analysis of the edited score (held at Oxford University Press) that, as we established, often omits and modifies the authentic annotations.

Studying these notes/annotations we are able, in fact, to understand how much attention Walton devoted to informing the orchestra and the soloist of the different "atmospheres" that he wanted to concerto to evoke: *sognando*, *sognando con molto espress.*, *arditamente*, *deliberatamente*, *giocoso leggiero*, *risoluto e quasi improvvisando* etc.

Moreover we know, thanks to the testimony of the composer and the violinist Yehudi Menhuin, that most of these were decided on by Jascha Heifetz, who brought about different changes to the soloist's score.

"In Walton's Violin Concerto, Heifetz indicates dynamics and directions in most intricate detail. Heifetz apparently attempts to reproduce his own interpretation of the performance. The small hairpin crescendos and decrescendos are not only for dynamic reasons, but also for coloristic expressions that come from expressive vibratos. These markings infect the music marked sognando with Heifetz's feverish musical sense....In the opening phrase of the first movement, Heifetz adds small hairpin crescendos and decrescendos to almost every note. But if the violinist follows these dynamics literally, the resulting sound is unnatural. Listening to the recording, Heifetz's use of dynamics seems to indicate a coloristic expression that corresponds to his use of vibrato."[58]

During the scoring of the concerto Walton repeatedly revealed himself as sincerely disposed to the violinist's requests and suggestions. In fact he'd visited Heifetz in America for the purpose of facilitating a more fluid collaboration.

The composer always kept Heifetz well informed, even pertaining to the smallest variation made to the score and Walton came to give the violinist his full faith when it occurred that he was unable to be present at the first performance. His confidence in Heifetz is demonstrated clearly by the second part of the letter Walton wrote on October 15, 1939 (the beginning of which was related earlier):

As for your alteration, I approve of it & send you some alternatives on a separate sheet, which pray heaven, a well-meaning, if unmusical censor, won't obliterate under the misapprehension that is a code! The only other suggestion I've made (in the 1st movement) is also in it.

Going through the parts, I have come across several mistakes in the full score, also here and there I've made a few alterations in the scoring which will, I trust be all to the good. They are notably as follows

3 bars after 1 the Cl & Vlc made identical with the similar phrase you have in the coda.

After 3 an additional Horn part (3rd) for safety!
After 6 changes in the Harp to make it more practical.
Before 17 in the cello part
Before 17 in the harp & Timpani.

---

[58] Mioi Takeda, *The Secrets of Jascha Heifet's Playing Style as Revealed Through His Editing of Works,* by Walton,Korngold and Waxman, City University of New York (2000), pp. 176.

I decided to hold on the Horn chord (2nd bar) for 4 bars, as as (sic) it stands, it is just a little to (sic) abrupt a bar . It will hardly be heard, rather as if it was sustained by the piano pedal.

In the "Trio" added the side-drum as I think it will give a little more kick & for the same reason after 55 onwards
Before 64 I've added the Timpani & slightly altered the Harp part.

There are other small details hardly worth going into a (sic) length which you will doubtless notice.

I am sending direct to Redding score bound & signed in one volume, as far as I can see, it is correct & incidentally so are the parts, as I've been most carefully through. The other score for the conductor & the parts are very (unreadable) New York. These parts are yours (and if) they have not already been done, you might have them stamped with your name. Will you return me the score recently sent you (in 2 vols) as it is incorrect & will need revising. Also could you at the same time send me a Photostat copy of your violin part as you will be playing it. I ask this, as we wish to get it in print (proofs only, not to be published till the date you stipulate) before the cost of printing becomes prohibitive.

I must confess I feel a bit nervous about a 1st performance at which I'm not there. It hasn't happened to me before, accordingly I give you my full permission to take any alterations you may find necessary, when you hear it on the orchestra. I've tried to make an orchestration as fool-proof as possible, but even there, it will need extremely careful playing, especially in the 2nd movement. Here a few suggestions.

Bar 2 it might better (sic) to have the 1st violins playing with the solo part for the one bar only and similarly at 28 & 4 bars after 33.

The Xylophone at 34 may be a bit much & be better out altogether. This refers also to the passage at 46. One before 66 the brass may be better " con sord"

At 73 & 1 bar before it may be more of a contrast to cut out the 'celli & let them enter with the Fagotto on the 2nd crotchet of the 9th bar after 73. In Cadenza after 75 the Gong & Bass drum may also be better out the way.

At 82 you might try this passage with 2 piccolos instead of Flutes it would be I suspect, brighter & more military (it was written when conscription was enforced! But perhaps far too shrill for the solo, especially in the bars after 83 but they could be played an octave lower & change back to 2 flutes at 84.

These are the only points I can think of, and I do trust that it will turn out well, if even only for the reason that I've slave like a black to get is as perfect as possible for you.

Excuse this very long letter & with best wishes for a successful first performance.

Kindest regards to Mrs. Heifetz and yourself
Yours ever
William Walton
P.S. It may be best, as I've done successfully in my Viola Concerto to cut down the strings while the solo is playing to

Vl.I 6 desks 12 players
Vl.II 5 desks 10 players
Vla. 4 desks 8 players
Vlc. 3 desks 6 players
Cb. 4 desks 4 players

& use the full body of strings only for the "tutti's"

This letter (which we have reproduced in its entirety) is probably one of the most interesting of all the documents concerning the Violin Concerto. Here, as in the manuscript, there is a direction that no scholar until now has brought to light: "conscription." By this Walton clearly communicated the origin of the march theme of the third movement, composed during his experience in the military.

Using this letter, written only shortly before the first performance, it is possible to reconstruct the final corrections brought to the score, establish the nature of the rapport between Walton and Heifetz and understand the absolute determination of the composer in his desire to realize a solo part moulded to the "violinism" of the great virtuoso.

"In 1938 Arnold Bax had written for Heifetz a concerto which the violinist effectively rejected and never played, quite possibly because it was not sufficiently virtuosic. Walton made every effort to ensure that his own concerto did not suffer a similar fate."[59]

Walton, with his Violin Concerto, celebrated technical grandeur, exemplified by Heifetz, and by Heifetz Walton was inspired to express, to the greatest lengths, his compositional abilities.

---

[59] Stephen Loyd William, *Walton: Muse of Fire*, Rochester, NY, Boydell Press (2001). pp.165.

As we have had the occasion to understand in the course of this analysis the violinist by no means represents the only influence on the work's development. "This concerto has inevitably invited comparisons with Elgar's Violin Concerto, principally because they share the unusual key of B minor, through which each expresses 'a peculiarly personal and introspective' mood, and also because of the accompanied cadenzas towards the ends of their finales. But even though the Walton cadenza may have been suggested by the Elgar, there are a number of differences between the two."[60]

The two cadenzas differ, above all, in length. Elgar's is notably longer than Walton's. Both recall themes from preceding movements within the concerto (the first movement in Walton and the second in Elgar). Yet while the solo violin of Elgar "Caresses them, lingers lovingly over them and finally bids them a fond farewell"[61] that of Walton's concerto "can afford no such indulgences, nor can his orchestra, and while both elaborate on earlier themes, they are firmly anchored to a dominant pedal , to careful barring and even suggested metronome markings."[62]

Despite the numerous differences the two concertos share the employment of an intense lyricism and the same fundamental harmonic choices, that of beginning the work in the key of B minor and concluding in the key of B major.

In short we have revealed in the first movement of Walton's concerto that which could be a citation of a fragment of the second movement of Elgar's concerto (similar rhythmic design, (enharmonically) same notes, both in an almost extemporaneous style)

Rather, the distinctive choices of Walton's work are: the form "weights + measures" of the first measure, derived from the principles of the sonata form, the frequent use of augmentation and diminution, the use of a *scherzo* in the place of the traditional slow second movement, the presence, in the final movement (also operating on the principles of the sonata) of thematic material from the first movement. The soloist's score alludes to the employment of more disparate techniques: harmonics, pizzicato, double stops, chords, sounds off the bridge; the instrument is able, therefore, to express all its timbric and sonic possibilities.

Walton came into contact with traditional Neapolitan music during his long sojourns in Italy, first on the Amalfi coast with the Sitwells, then at

[60] Robert Meikle, da Stewart R. Craggs, *William Walton: Music and Literature*, Aldershot, Ashgate Publishing (1999), pp.83.
[61] Michael Kennedy, *Portrait of Elgar*, Oxford, Clarendon Press (1987), pp.250-1.
[62] Robert Meikle, da Stewart R. Craggs, *William Walton: Music and Literature*, Aldershot, Ashgate Publishing (1999),pp.83.

Ravello with Alice Wimborne. It was to influence his work. The second movement is, without a doubt, that which most exhibits this influence, for the presence of the tarantella dance and for thematic patterns clearly of Mediterranean origin, such as I C.

Two other factors conditioned the "character" of the concerto: Walton's love for Alice Wimborne and Walton's direct experience with the war.

The first of these factors determined the romantic character of the work, musically expressed through a pervasive lyricism while the second, the one that scholars have often left out, strongly conditioned the scoring of the last movement whose march theme, as Walton himself maintains, was written during his military tour.

It therefore appears evident that every musical decision made by Walton didn't depend exclusively on compositional criteria but rather these decisions are solidly linked to external factors: virtuosity from his collaboration with Heifetz, lyricism from his love for Alice, the dance from his stays in Italy, the march from his experiences with the war in England.

Again, the place, the people, the interactions were what guided the hand of the composer. The concerto for violin and orchestra by William Walton remains among the most fascinating of the entire repertoire of works for violin, a testimony to how a "small voice" could emerge as among the most powerful in the history of 20th Century music.

APPENDIX

Documented here are a number of unpublished writings relating to the concerto, collected during research. In all cases they belong to notable performers and composers who had close involvement with Walton and his music.

Hans Werner Henze: German composer, one of the most important European composers of the post-war era.

In 1952 he and Walton met in Italy. Their close friendship lasted throughout their lives.

Salvatore Accardo: Italian concert violinist and teacher. He is considered one of Italy's greatest 20th century talents. In 1991 he recorded Walton's Violin Concerto for REGIS (with the London Symphony Orchestra, directed by Richard Hickox). Accardo and Aldo Ferraresi are the only Italian performers to have recorded the concerto.

James Ehnes: Canadian concerto violinist. Ehnes won a Grammy in the Best Instrumental Soloist(s) Performance (with Orchestra) category for his *Barber/Korngold/Walton: Violin Concertos* album. In 2006 he recorded Walton's concerto for ONYX (with the Vancouver Symphony Orchestra directed by Bramwell Tovey).

Matthew Jones: English concert violist and violinist. Winner of the prize for the most promising British entrant in the 2003 Lionel Tertis International Viola Competition. Winner of the Walton Fellowship in 2006.

Fenella Humphreys English concert violinist. Winner of the Philip and Dorothy Green Award for Young Concert Artists 2005. In 2006 he performed Walton's Violin Concerto for the opening of the Teatro Greco theater on La Mortella, Ischia.

Hans Werner Henze

After World War II I studied composition at the Heidelberg Conservatory, which in those years was occupied by American troops. The individual responsible for culture invited me to listen to some of his recordings. He had recently acquired a new piece, William Walton's Violin Concerto, recorded by Jascha Heifetz. It was the first concerto for violin and orchestra that I'd ever heard. I'd never encountered anything similar and I remember being enchanted by the elegance of the melodic and thematic composition. I found the piece to be charming and when, years later, I wrote my first Violin Concerto I most certainly had that piece's waltonian tessitura in mind.

On first hearing the piece one could speak of classicism, but I would avoid this term ... maybe it's better to say romanticism, its more adapted to the music's tone He created a quite elegant and seductive musical language that avoids scandalous solutions. He knows how to express an idea that was freely erotic yet never vulgar. The elegant style is for Walton the point of departure of any musical construction.

Many years later, in 1952, I moved to Italy, on the island of Ischia, where by chance I rented a house not far from Sir William's villa.

I didn't know that it was him. I thought it was Vaughan Williams! It took me some time to realize my mistake! He knew that there was a German composer on the island who was of the young anti-waltonian generation. Yet I was most certainly neither anti Waltonian nor anti Vaughan Williams! We finally met in person for the occasion of receiving the poet W.H. Auden.

And so it was that I was able to once again hear the Violin Concerto. I still didn't have a record player and in that time tape players and CD's didn't exist. There was, however, William Walton, a truly charming person.

Gentle and timid, it was difficult for him to open up to others. Yet he and I were able to strike up an alliance based on a rare faith and kindness almost immediately. We were like brothers and we remained that way for our whole lives. We sought the same aesthetic ideas without grand discourses.

Then I left Ischia and went to live first in Naples and then Rome, this meant seeing each other less. Nevertheless we continued to remain in touch and we followed each other's careers with great attention.

I remember when in 1954 he came to Naples to assist in the presentation of my opera Boulevard Solitude at the Teatro San Carlo. After the concerto he said "Dear boy in ten years time you will be a world success!" From that moment I've tried to make his prophecy a reality. I so admire Sir William.

Salvatore Accardo

I first heard William Walton's Violin Concerto through the historical Jascha Heifetz recording. I was struck by Heifetz's playing ... that concerto worked so well with his approach. His technique was truly wonderful, resoundingly clear and solid. Moreover it possessed an almost Spartan cantabilità. He was not a violinist who would let himself hang out!

Walton's genius is colossal! The concerto was not written for a soloist with accompaniment. The violin's timbric and sonic possibilities are treated in their entirety with the violin serving as part of the orchestra. I believe that it's the difficulty of the solo and orchestral parts that are responsible for this extraordinary concerto's not being played more. .

Only an exceptional virtuoso, expert orchestra and highly capable director are able to perform it!

In my view the best interpreters of this concerto are the English orchestras, who possess a sound that is different, for example, from that of the beautiful but less malleable German orchestras.

Every composition leaves you so much ... in is an incredible form of enrichment. I always say that the most important thing in a musician's development is the meeting of other musicians, composers and the mark left by the compositions themselves. This concerto, beyond the fact of its technique and violinistic approach, moved me deeply. If you aren't moved the public will not be moved and with Walton's Violin Concerto this happens from the first bar.

James Ehnes

William Walton's Violin Concerto is, in my opinion, one of the great masterpieces of its genre.

I think that Walton's reputation in general is unfairly overshadowed by Elgar from the older generation, and Britten from the slightly younger generation. His music was certainly criticized in the middle part of the last century for being "old-fashioned", but I think his unique voice can now be fully appreciated, now that time has given us some sense of perspective regarding music of the 20th century. I would hope that his lasting reputation will be as one of the great composers of the 1900's.

The reputation of the violin concerto is somewhat overshadowed by Walton's own viola concerto, though it seems that the violin concerto is finally beginning to receive the attention it deserves. The viola concerto was certainly enormously influential and has enjoyed intense popularity since its creation in 1929, but the violin concerto is, in my opinion, an equally impressive work. It has all of the qualities one would wish to find in a violin concerto - beautiful soaring melodies, rich orchestral accompaniment, and certainly a great deal of virtuoso firepower. The violin writing is quite unique; some of the specific technical challenges are unlike any others found in the violin's repertoire. I have often wondered how much influence Jascha Heifetz had in the writing of the solo parts. Some of the writing in the 2nd movement particularly gives me the impression of being composed for a very particular pair of hands!

I think the influence of the 3rd movement of Elgar's violin concerto upon the 3rd movement of Walton's concerto cannot be overlooked. It seems obvious to me that the "accompanied cadenza" figures towards the end of the Walton concerto must draw some of their inspiration from the stunning and extremely unique cadenza in the final pages of Elgar's concerto. It would have, of course, been impossible for any British composer of Walton's generation to have remained uninfluenced by Elgar!

It has been my experience that Walton's concerto is an extremely effective piece with audiences, and it is always a great challenge and pleasure for the violinist, the conductor, and the orchestra. I hope that its popularity continues to rise, and that I will have many opportunities in the future to perform this wonderful work.

Matthew Jones

My love affair with Walton's Violin Concerto began, as so often happens, in unexpected circumstances. I was beginning my second attempt at a year's postgraduate study at the Royal College of Music after two years of unfathomable frustration, overcoming an injury problem in my right arm and wrist which left me unable to play for more than a few minutes per day.

At the stage of returning to the RCM, I was able to manage to practice for maybe an hour each day, and was studying with a teacher who usually demanded five hours of practice from pupils. A month into the academic year, he announced that he had a piece he thought would be good for me to learn, referring mainly to the opening page of the concerto, as it turned out, with its expressive writing which is hard work for the left hand but not so much for the right. Excited to discover a new work, I bought a recording and soon got extremely scared – how, in my delicate state of rehabilitation, could I possibly be in a fit state to attempt the fiendish passagework? How could I learn it fast enough? Yet, at the same time, I knew I'd discovered a gem of a piece which I couldn't wait to master, however long it may take me.

The influence of Heifetz, or rather Walton's idea of how a piece should be in order to be worthy of consideration by Heifetz, was immediately apparent, but it was a recording by Ida Haendel which persuaded me of the work's genius. Although it could be argued that the later movements are not quite so comfortably played, her version of the first movement is, for me, by far the most moving of all versions recorded to date. Her ability to sustain phrases and make a simple gesture tug at the heart strings is a perfect match to the musical content.

With characteristic modesty, Walton's letters show that he was less than sure that his piece would be worthy of the great Heifetz, which makes it all the more extraordinary that so very few changes were made by the dedicatee, despite being given a fairly free hand to do so. The composer had also had relatively little experience of writing for the instrument and had never played, yet the result, despite its huge difficulties, feels naturally violinistic. As a player, it challenges one to explore technical areas seldom visited, yet is always accessible enough that one knows it should at least be possible to become comfortable! It has that rare quality that makes one want to work on purely technical issues on the violin in order to become able to play the piece: personally speaking, it inspired me to go back to basics in many aspects of technique for both hands, with the inspiration of knowing that, having mastered the aspect of technique, I'd be a step closer to being able to perform the concerto!

I chose Ravello as the destination for a winter holiday some years ago in which I wanted to escape, alone, from London and my hectic lifestyle, partly due to my knowledge of how the place had inspired Walton in his writing of this concerto. The fact that I bumped into Lady Walton at Naples airport completely by chance en route seemed somehow a sign that this visit had been a good idea! Walking in the Villa Cimbrone, where he stayed and worked, it became clear how the opening 'sognando' theme of the first movement could have entered the composer's mind: although it has many of the trademarks of his melodic writing, there is something about it which sets it apart from many of his other melodies, perhaps in the 'question and answer' nature of the phrase (though the answer is still open-ended, of course), perhaps in the choice of intervals.

The final movement's genius, to me, lies in Walton's compositional technique of superimposing the rhythmic theme over the lyrical one in a perfectly formed but often surprising way, most noticeably in the second occurrence of the lyrical theme where the solo violin soars high with a slurred version of the opening bassoon theme, creating one of the most poignant moments of the concerto when the melody jumps back down by an octave. Here, as so often in his music, Walton shows perfect judgment in his use of register and intervals.

Some years after my initial discovery of, and perhaps (healthy!) obsession with the violin concerto, and after a complete recovery from my injuries, I began to play the viola, and have performed Walton's concerto for that instrument with orchestra on numerous occasions. The viola concerto rightly has its place in the repertoire of most concert violists, and I hope that its counterpart for violin will continue to inspire many violinists to face its challenges and give the piece the widespread popularity it deserves.

Fenella Humphreys

I first heard the Walton concerto in my teens at a performance given by Joshua Bell at the Proms. I remember being mesmerised by the work, particularly by the way the music danced, the unique timbres created by the orchestration, and the interaction between soloist and orchestra. I finally had the opportunity to learn it a few years later when I was invited to perform for the opening of the Greek Theatre in Ischia.

As I began to work on the concerto, both the beauty and the technical difficulty struck me equally. However it was immediately clear that the technique serves the music rather than vice versa. There are no fireworks that are gratuitously there, purely to be impressive, and everything to me makes musical sense.

I find it to be a very personal work. It does not seem to fit into the English tradition particularly, when one thinks of its predecessors, for example Elgar (interestingly also in B minor) and Delius. There is no feeling of the English 'idyll' style of writing here. The language seems to me far more brilliant and sparkling. Even in the many singing and 'sognando' sections, the mood seems far more hazy than could be conjured up by Elgarian images of rolling English hills.

The large scale structure is unlike any other violin concerto I can think of. Although there is no slow movement as such, the mixture of slow and fast as well as dreamy cadenza-passages in each movement balances the work as a whole.

The rhythmic language is often complex in the work, though at the same time even the most rhythmically complicated passages dance in a way that makes them clearly understandable as a listener.

It was definitely a challenging concerto to learn. There were the obvious Heifetz-inspired technical passages to get to grips with.   More importantly though I find it is also tricky to find the right balances – for example to make the rhythms dance without becoming caricatured, to make the sognando passages dreamy and lovely without becoming over-sentimental, and to find the searching character in the cadenza passages without becoming lost.

To perform it is a real joy.   The power of the rhythmical energy in the orchestra is incredibly exciting.   The writing also creates the perfect carpet in the orchestra over which to sing.   Although the violin is obviously the solo instrument, there is such a sense of chamber music rhythmically and melodically.   The interaction between soloist and orchestra which I found so thrilling the first time I heard the concerto is even more satisfying to be a part of.

Although the concerto was written before Walton had thoughts of Ischia, to be able to perform it at his home and for Lady Walton was a huge honour.   I was fortunate to have the opportunity to practice in the music room where Walton had composed which alone would have been inspiration enough.   Added to this, performing in the open-air theatre to an audience almost in darkness (the garden lit only by coloured lights) gave me the freedom to feel I could get right inside the work and really speak the emotions, throwing them out into the stars.

BIBLIOGRAPHY

The researching of bibliographic material, scores and manuscripts was conducted through:

- Archivio Fondazione William Walton , La Mortella
- Beinecke Rare Book and Manuscript Library , Università di Yale
- Biblioteca del Conservatorio Santa Cecilia
- Biblioteca dell'Accademia Santa Cecilia
- Biblioteca Nazionale Centrale di Roma
- Biblioteca di Storia della Musica del Dipartimento di Studi Glottoantropologici e Discipline Musicali dell'Università la Sapienza
- JSTOR
- ProQuest Information and Learning Database

Music History, England

Enciclopedia della musica UTET: Storia della musica, Volume Terzo: Dal 1839 alla fine dell'Ottocento, Alberto Basso: "Le Isole britanniche" pp.1339-1345

Enciclopedia della musica UTET: Storia della musica, Volume Quarto: Il primo Novecento, Carlo Benzi; Stefano A.E. Leoni :Gli stili nazionali del Novecento: "Britten e la musica Inglese del primo Novecento" pp.79-80

Enciclopedia della musica Einaudi: Il Novecento I Bojan Buhic: Le tradizioni nazionali "Gran Bretagna" pp. 94-95

Donal Jay Grout, Storia della Musica in Occidente: La fine di un'epoca: Inghilterra pp.672-673 ; Il ventesimo secolo:Inghilterra pp. 699-703

Edward Lockspeiser *Trends in Modern English Music,* The Musical Quarterly,MQ,Vol.28, No.1 (Jan.,1942), pp.1-13

Eric Blom *Music in England* ,La Nuova Italia (1966) pp.220

Percy M. Young, *A history of British music* , W. W. Norton (1967)

Otto Karolyi *Modern British Music , The Second British Musical Renaissance- From Elgar to P. Maxwell Devies* , Fairleigh Dickinson University Press (1994)

Andrew Blake *The Land without Music* Manchester University Press (1997)

Meirion Hughes, Robert Stradling   *The English Musical Renaissance 1840-1940. Constructing a National Music,*   Manchester University Press , Second Edition (2001)

History of the Concerto

Arnaldo Bonaventura, *Storia del violino, dei violinisti e della musica per violino*, Ed.Lampi di Stampa (1993)
Robin Stowell,*The Cambridge Companion to the Violin*, Cambridge University Press (1993)
Michael Thomas Roeder   *A history of the concerto*   Amadeus Press (2003)
Mark Katz *The Violin: A Research and Information Guide*, Routledge (2006)

Charles Stanford

Enciclopedia della musica UTET:Le Biografie:Vol.VII ,pp.432-433
The New Groove Dictionary of Music and Musicians
Herbert Howells   *Charles Villiers Stanford (1852-1924). An Address at His Centenary*   Proceedings of the Royal Musical Association, 79th Sess. (1952-1953), pp.19-31.

Edward Elgar

Enciclopedia della musica UTET:Le Biografie:Vol.II, pp.641-643
The New Groove Dictionary of Music and Musicians
Ernest Newman. *Elgar's Violin Concerto,* The Musical Times,MT, Vol.41, No.812. (Oct.1, 1910), pp.631-634.
Eugene Ysaye. *M.Ysaye and the Elgar Violin Concerto,* The Musical Times, MT,Vol.54, No.839. (Jan.1,1913), pp.19-20
W.H. Reed. *Elgar's Violin Concerto,* Music and Letters, Vol.16, No.1. (Jan.,1935), pp.30-36
Donald Francis Tovey. *Essays in Music Analysis, Vol.3 Concertos* Oxford University Press (1936),pp. 152-58
Herbert Byard. *Introduction, Violin Concerto,* The Concerto Edited by Ralph Hill, Pellican Books (1952) pp. 252-58
Robert Magidoff   *Yehudi Menuhin: The story of the man and the musician* Westport, Conn.: Greenwood Press, 1973, (c1955), pp.150-55, 268-9
David Ewen. *The World of Twentieth Century Music,* Prentice Hall (1970), pp. 252-53

Yehudi Menuhin. *Sir Edward Elgar, My Musical Grandfather,* Elgar
    Society (1976)
Yehudi Menuhin. *Unfinished Journey* London MacDonald and Jane's
    (1977), pp. 120-21
Robert Philip. *The Recordings of Edward Elgar (1857-1934): Authenticity
    and Performance Practice,* Early Music, Vol.12, No.4, The Early
    Piano I. (Nov.,1984), pp.481-485, 487-489
Michael Kennedy. *Portrait of Elgar,* Oxford: Clarendon Press (1987),pp.
    192-211

Samuel Coleridge-Taylor

Enciclopedia della musica UTET:Le Biografie:Vol.II,pp.288
The New Groove Dictionary of Music and Musicians
Mr. Coleridge Taylor The Musical Times, Vol. 50 , No 793 (Mar.1 , 1909)
    pp.153-158
Samuel Coleridge-Taylor. Born August 15, 1875. Died September 1,1912
    The Musical Times, Vol.53, No.836. (Oct.1,1912), pp.637-639
Percy M. Young. *Samuel Coleridge-Taylor, 1875-1912,* The Musical
    Times, Vol.116, No.1590. (Aug.,1975), pp.703-705
Sidney Butterworth, *Coleridge-Taylor: New Facts for Old Ficition,* The
    Musical Times,MT, Vol.130,No. 1754. (Apr.,1989),pp.202-204
Geofrrey Self. *Coleridge-Taylor and the Orchestra,* Black Music Research
    Journal, Vol.21, No.2,Samuel Coleridge-Taylor. (Autumn,2001), pp.261-
    282.

Frederick Delius

Enciclopedia della musica UTET:Le Biografie:Vol. II, pp.444
The New Groove Dictionary of Music and Musicians
Donald Francis Tovey   *Essays in Music Analysis, Vol.3 Concertos* Oxford
    University Press (1936), 203-5
Ralph Hill. *Frederick Delius*   Music of our Time, ed. A.L. Bacharach,
    Harmondsworth (1946),pp. 30-43
Arthur Hutchings *Introduction, Violin Concerto*   The Concerto Edited by
    Ralph Hill, Pellican Books (1952), pp.261-63,270-75
Hubert Foss. *The Instrumental Music of Frederick Delius,* Tempo, New
    Ser., No.26, Delius Number. Winter (1952-1953),pp.30-37.
Christopher Redwood. *A Delius Companion.* London: John Calder (1980),
    pp.252-262

Ralph Vaughan Williams

Enciclopedia della musica UTET:Le Biografie:Vol.VIII ,pp..173-176
The New Groove Dictionary of Music and Musicians
William Mann. *Introduction, Vaughan Williams: Concerto Accademico*
The Concerto, Edited by Ralph Hill, Penguin Books (1952) pp. 400-05,422-25
Michael Kennedy. *The Works of Ralph Vaughan Williams* Oxford University Press,2nd edition (1980), Clarendon Paperback (1992) pp.216
Stephen Banfield. *Hickox Conducts Vaughan Williams* Cd booklet (EMI)

Arthur Somervell

Enciclopedia della musica UTET:Le Biografie:Vol. VII, pp..362
The New Groove Dictionary of Music and Musicians
Donald Francis Tovey. *Essays in Music Analysis, Vol.3 Concertos* Oxford University Press (1936), pp. 158-164

Arnold Bax

Enciclopedia della musica UTET:Le Biografie
The New Groove Dictionary of Music and Musicians
Guy Rickards Tempo, New Ser., No 180 (Mar.1992) pp. 56-58
Otto Karolyi. *Modern British Music* pp.21

Benjamin Britten

Enciclopedia della musica UTET:Le Biografie. Vol. I, pp.700-702
The New Groove Dictionary of Music and Musicians
Scott Goddard, *Benjamin Britten Music of our Time*, ed. A.L. Bacharach , Harmondsworth (1946),pp. 209-218
David Ewen *The World of Twentieth Century Music,* Prentice Hall (1970),pp.112-15
Suzanne Robinson, *"An English Composer Sees America": Benjamin Britten and the North American Press,1939-42.* American Music, Vol.15, No.3. (Autumn, 1997), pp.326-28

William Walton

Enciclopedia della musica UTET:Le Biografie: Vol. VIII, pp.394

The New Groove Dictionary of Music and Musicians

Hubert J. Foss *William Walton* The Chesterian, xi (1930),pp.175-81

Alan Frank. *The Music of William Walton,* The Chesterian, xx (1939),pp.153-6

Hubert J. Foss. *William Walton,* The Musical Quarterly, MQ, xxvi (1940),pp. 456-66

Frank Merrick. *Walton's Concerto for Violin and Orchestra* The Music Review 2 (1941) pp.309-18

Edwin Evans. *William Walton,* The Musical Times, MT, lxxxv (1944),pp. 329-32,364-8

Colin Mason. *William Walton,* British Music of our Time, ed. A.L. Bacharach , Harmondsworth (1946),pp. 137-49

Kenneth Avery. *William Walton*, Music and Letters, ML , xxviii (1947),pp. 1-11

Frank Howes. *The music of William Walton,* Vol. I , Oxford University Press (1947),pp. 59-76

Herbert Murril. *Walton's Violin Sonata*, Music and Letters, ML, (1950),pp. 208-15

Robert Magidoff. *Yehudi Menuhin: The story of the man and the musician* Westport, Conn.: Greenwood Press, 1973, (c1955),pp.280-81

Arthur Jacobs. *Passing Notes*, The Gramophone, (1962) , pp. 373

Peter J. Pirie. *Scapino. The Development of William Walton,* The Musical Times,MT, Vol.105, No.1454. (Apr.,1964), pp.258-259

David Ewen. *The World of Twentieth Century Music,* Prentice Hall (1970),pp. 880-90

Christopher Palmer. *Walton's Film Music* , The Musical Times, MT, cxiii (1972),pp.249-52

Stewart Craggs. *A Walton Pot-Pourri,* The Musical Times, MT, cxiii (1972), pp.253-4

Hugh Ottaway. *Walton's First Symphony* , The Musical Times, MT, cxiii (1972),pp. 254-7

Hugh Ottaway. *Walton Adapted,* The Musical Times, MT, cxv (1974),pp.582

Yehudi Menuhin. *Unfinished Journey* London MacDonald and Jane's (1977), pp.158-59, 316-17

Bayan Northcott. *In Search of Walton* , The Musical Times, MT, cxxiii (1982), pp.179-84

Christopher Palmer. *Sir William Walton* , The Musical Times, MT, cxxiv

(1983),pp. 316

Anne Marie de Zeeuw. *Tonality and the Concertos of William Walton* diss., U. of Texas, Austin, (1983)

Neil Tierney. *William Walton: His Life and Music* London: Robert Hale (1984), pp.83-92

Susana Walton. *William Walton: Behind the Façade* Oxford University Press (1988), pp.87-92, 140-41, 162-63, 170-71, 180-81, 188-89, 216-19, 226-27

Michael Kennedy. *Portrait of Walton.* Oxford University Press (1989), pp.96-107

Herbert R.Axelrod. *Heifetz*, Paganiniana (1990), pp.368-9, 374-77, 384, 390-5, 418-9, 428-9

Stewart R Craggs. *William Walton: Music and Literature.* Ashgate Publishing (1999), pp.67–108

Stephen Lloyd. *William Walton: Muse of Fire Press* Boydell Press (2001)

Humphrey Burton, Maureen Murray. *William Walton: The Romantic Loner: A Centenary Portrait Album* Oxford University Press (2002)

Malcolm Hayes. *The Selected Letters of William Walton.* Faber and Faber (2002)

Mioi Takeda. *The Secrets of Jascha Heifetz's Playing Style as Revealed Through His Editing of Works by Walton, Korngold and Waxman.* The City University of New York (2002)

Scores

Edward Elgar

Concerto per violino e orchestra in Si minore, op.61, Novello & Co Ltd.

Frederick Delius

Concerto per violino e orchestra, Stainer & Bell.

Benjamin Britten

Concerto per violino e orchestra Op.15 , Boosey and Hawkes

William Walton

Concerto per violino e orchestra in Si minore, Oxford University Press

Concerto per violino e orchestra in Si minore, Manoscritto FRKF 597, Beinecke Rare Book and Manuscript Library , Università di Yale

Official Sites

Edward Elgar
http://www.elgar.org/
http://www.elgarfoundation.org/
Frederick Delius
http://www.delius.org.uk/
Ralph Vaughan Williams
http://www.rvwsociety.com/
William Walton
http://www.williamwalton.net/
http://www.waltontrust.org.uk/
http://www.lamortella.it/
Benjamin Britten
http://www.brittenpears.org/

DISCOGRAPHY

Charles Villiers Stanford Concerto per violino e orchestra in Re maggiore, Op.74
- Anthony Markwood
  BBC Scottish Symphony Orchestra
  Martyn Brabbins
  HYPERION

Edward Elgar   Concerto per violino e orchestra in Si minore, op.61
- Marie Hall
  Symphony Orchestra
  Edward Elgar
  LTM
- Alfredo Campoli
  London Philharmonic Orchestra
  Adrian Boult
  BEULAH
- Aldo Ferraresi
  Orchestra Sinfonica RAI di Milano
  Milton Forstat
  COMITATO GRANDI MAESTRI
- Albert Sammons
  New Queen's Hall Orchestra
  Henry Wood
  NAXOS
- Hilary Hahn
  London Philharmonic Orchestra
  Colin Davis
  DEUTSCHE GRAMMOPHONE
- Jascha Heifetz
  London Symphony Orchestra
  Malcom Sargent
  NAXOS
- Kyung Wha Chung
  London Philharmonic Orchestra

Georg Solti
DECCA
• Nigel Kennedy
London Philharmonic Orchestra
Vernon Handley
EMI
• Salvatore Accardo
London Symphony Orchestra
Richard Hickox
REGIS
• Yehudi Menuhin
New Philharmonia Orchestra
Adrian Boult
EMI
• Yehudi Menuhin
London Symphony Orchestra
Edward Elgar
EMI

Samuel Coleridge-Taylor Concerto for Violin and Orchestra in G Major, Op.80

• Anthony Markwood
BBC Scottish Symphony Orchestra
Martyn Brabbins
HYPERION

Friederick Delius Concerto for Violin and Orchestra

• Albert Sammons
Liverpool Philharmonic Orchestra
Malcom Sargent
NAXOS
• Tasmin Little
Welsh National Opera Orchestra
Charles Mackerras
ARGO
• Yehudi Menuhin
Royal Philharmonic Orchestra
Meredith Davies
EMI

Ralph Vaughan Williams Concerto for Violin and Orchestra in D Minor "Concerto Accademico"
- Kenneth Sillito
London Symphony Orchestra
Bryden Thomson
CHANDOS
- Bradley Creswick
Northern Sinfonia of England
Richard Ickox
EMI

Arthur Somervell Concerto for Violin and Orchestra in G Minor
- Anthony Markwood
BBC Scottish Symphony Orchestra
Martyn Brabbins
HYPERION

Arnold Bax Concerto for Violin and Orchestra
- Lydia Mordkovitch
London Philharmonic
Bryden Thomson
CHANDOS

Benjamin Britten Concerto for Violin and Orchestra Op.15
- Daniel Hope
BBC Symphony Orchestra
Paul Watkins
Warner Classics
- Ida Haendel
Bournemouth Symphony Orchestra
Paavo Berglund
EMI
- Maxim Vengerov
London Symphony Orchestra
Mstislav Rostropovich
EMI
- Sergej Azizian
Copenhagen Philharmonic Orchestra
Giordano Bellicampi
SCANDINAVIAN CLASSIC

William Walton Concerto for Violin and Orchestra in B Minor

- Aaron Rosand
Florida Philharmonic Orchestra
James Judd
HARMONIA MUNDI
- Akiko Suwanai
City of Birmingham Symphony Orchestra
Sakari Oramo
PHILIPS
- Aldo Ferraresi
Orchestra Sinfonica RAI di Milano
Milton Forstat
COMITATO GRANDI MAESTRI
- Berl Senofsky
The New Zealand Symphony Orchestra
William Walton
BRIDGE
- Camilla Wicks
Oslo Philharmonic
Yuri Simonov
SIMAX
- Dong-Suk Kang
English Northern Philarmonia
Paul Daniel
NAXOS
- Erick Friedman
Stockholm Philharmonic
Everett Lee
- Ida Haendel
Bournemouth Symphony Orchestra
Paavo Berglund
EMI
- James Ehnes
Vancouver Symphony Orchestra
Bramwell Tovey
ONYX
- Jascha Heifetz
Cincinnati Symphony Orchestra
Eugene Goossens
RCA

- Jascha Heifetz
Philharmonia Orchestra
William Walton
RCA
- Joshua Bell
Baltimore Symphony Orchestra
David Zinman
DECCA
- Kyung Wha Chung
London Symphony Orchestra
Andre Previn
DECCA
- Lydia Mordkovitch
London Philharmonic
Jan Latham-Koenig
CHANDOS
- Nigel Kennedy
Royal Philarmonic Orchestra
Andre Previn
EMI
- Salvatore Accardo
London Symphony Orchestra
Richard Hickox
REGIS
- Sergej Azizian
Copenhagen Philharmonic Orchestra
Giordano Bellicampi
SCANDINAVIAN CLASSIC
- Tasmin Little
Bournemouth Symphony Orchestra
Andrew Litton
DECCA
- Yehudi Menuhin
Philharmonia Orchestra
William Walton
EMI

FILMOGRAPHY

Edward Elgar
- Ken Russell   *Elgar*   (1962)   BBC

Frederick Delius
- Ken Russell   *A Song of Summer* (1968)   BBC

William Walton
- Tony Palmer   *At the Haunted End of the Day*   (1981)   DECCA
- Paolo Petrocelli   *William Walton. Il fascino di una voce fievole, storia di un concerto per violino*   (2007)